Reminiscences of

Vice Admiral Gerald F. Bogan

U.S. Navy (Retired)

U.S. Naval Institute

Annapolis, Maryland

1970/1986

DECLARATION OF TRUST

The undersigned does hereby appoint and designate as his (her) Trustee herein, the Secretary-Treasurer and Publisher of the United States Naval Institute to perform and discharge the following duties, powers, and privileges in connection with the possession and use of a certain taped interview between the undersigned and the Oral History Department of the United States Naval Institute.

(1) As an <u>Open</u> transcript. It may be read (or the tape audited) by qualified researchers upon presentation of proper credentials as determined by the Trustee.

(2) It is expressly understood that in giving this authorization, I am in no way precluded from placing such restrictions as I may desire upon use of the interview at any time during my lifetime, nor does this authorization in any way affect my rights to the copyright of any literary expressions that may be contained in the interview.

Witness my hand and seal this 17th day of December 1969

Gerald F. Bogan

I hereby accept and consent to the foregoing Declaration of Trust and the powers therein conferred upon me as Trustee:

R. E. Bowker Jr
Secretary-Treasurer and Publisher

Preface -- 1970

This manuscript is the result of a tape-recorded interview with Vice Admiral Gerald F. Bogan, USN (Ret.) at his home in La Jolla, California, on October 25, 1969. The interviewer was Commander Etta-Belle Kitchen, USN (Ret.) and the work was done for the Oral History office in the U.S. Naval Institute.

Admiral Bogan made only minor emendations and corrections to the manuscript. The reader is asked to bear in mind therefore that he is reading a transcript of the spoken word rather than the written word.

Preface -- 1986

The oral history transcript of Vice Admiral Bogan was one of the first to be published by the Naval Institute. As a result, some of the refinements that have later become standard parts of the format were not yet incorporated. In addition to those corrections made originally by Admiral Bogan himself, some slight editing has now been done in the interest of clarity and smoothness. A careful listening to the tapes of the oral history indicates that it was done over a two-day period. There is thus a break at a logical but arbitrarily selected place to indicate the division between interviews. The transcript has been annotated with footnotes to provide additional information, and the volume has been indexed in the format now standard for Naval Institute oral histories. The original version, which contains Admiral Bogan's handwritten corrections, is still on file at the Naval Institute.

VICE ADMIRAL GERALD F. BOGAN, U. S. NAVY (RETIRED)

Gerald Francis Bogan was born in Mackinac Island, Michigan, on 27 July 1894, son of James H. and Katherine Nash Bogan. He attended Lane Technical High School in Chicago before his appointment to the Naval Academy, Annapolis, Maryland, which he entered from the Ninth District of Illinois, on 15 June 1912. While a midshipman, he played class football, participated in boxing, and won his letter as a member of crew. Graduated and commissioned ensign on 3 June 1916, he received temporary promotion to lieutenant, both grades, during World War I, and subsequently advanced to the rank of rear admiral to date from 7 December 1942. On 28 December 1945, he was appointed vice admiral, to date from 2 February 1946, and was transferred to the retired list of the U.S. Navy in that rank on 1 February 1950.

After graduation from the Naval Academy in June 1916, he was assigned to the USS Vermont. The following October he reported for duty as instructor of enlisted men at the Naval Training Station, Great Lakes. Detached in March 1917, shortly prior to the United States' entry into World War I, he joined the USS Birmingham, in which he served as watch and gunnery officer while that cruiser was employed on escort of convoy duty in European waters throughout the war period.

In January 1919, after the Armistice, he was transferred to the USS Stribling, operating in Mediterranean and Adriatic waters, and a year later he joined the USS Hopewell to serve until May 1920 as engineer officer and later executive officer. He served next as executive officer of the USS Broome (DD-210), operating in the European and Asiatic areas, and in January 1922 became commanding officer of the U.S. Naval Radio Station, Russian Island, Vladivostok, Siberia. He returned that station to the Soviet forces after its decommissioning.

Returning to the Naval Academy in March 1923, he served as an instructor in the Department of Electrical Engineering and Physics until May 1924 when he was ordered to the Naval Training Station, Naval Operating Base, Hampton Roads, Virginia. After brief duty there he reported in August to the Naval Air Station, Pensacola, Florida, where he had flight training and was designated naval aviator on 16 March 1925. He then was ordered to Honolulu, Hawaii, to join Fighting Squadron One, based on the aircraft carrier Langley (CV-1), and served for a year as executive officer of that squadron, and in command from September 1926 until July 1928.

For two years he served as commanding officer of Squadron One and Wing Commander of Landplanes at the Naval Air Station, Pensacola, Florida, and from June 1930 until July 1931 commanded

Fighting Squadron Three, based on the USS Lexington (CV-2), later the USS Langley. That squadron won the aircraft efficiency award for excellence in bombing and gunnery with an annual merit 50% higher than the second place squadron. He next served as Commander Fighting Squadron One, of the USS Saratoga (CV-3), and in June 1932 was detached for shore duty as flight test officer at the Naval Air Station, Anacostia, D.C. In June 1934 he rejoined the Lexington, in which he served as assistant air officer until June 1935, and as air officer for a year thereafter.

He again had a tour of duty at the Pensacola Naval Air Station, this time as superintendent of aviation training until May 1937, and as executive officer until June 1938. He then joined the USS Yorktown (CV-5), in which he served for a year each as navigator and executive officer. In August 1940 he reported for duty in connection with the establishment of the naval air station at Miami, Florida, and commanded that station from its commissioning through the early months of World War II until October 1942.

He then took command of the USS Saratoga, which had been damaged in August 1942 and returned to Pearl Harbor for repairs. That carrier operated in the South Pacific in support of Guadalcanal capture and extension of advance bases in the Solomon Islands. Detached on 15 June 1943, he then served until 10 October as Commander Naval Air, Tenth Fleet, under Admiral Ernest J. King. The Tenth Fleet had no ships of its own but drew on air and surface forces of the Atlantic Fleet to combat the submarine menace. On 14 October 1943, he was designated Commander Fleet Air, Norfolk, Virginia, and on 18 January 1944, became Commander Carrier Division 25. Four months later he was transferred to command of Carrier Division 11, and on 5 February 1945, was transferred to command of Carrier Division Four. Following the Saipan operation, he became Commander Task Group 38.2 and served as a task group commander in Task Force 58/38 until the end of the war.

For outstanding service in those commands during widespread operations in the Pacific area, he was awarded the Legion of Merit, Distinguished Service Medal, gold star in lieu of the second Distinguished Service Medal, and the Navy Cross. The citations follow, in order of action for which received:

Legion of Merit: "For exceptionally meritorious conduct . . . as Commander of a Carrier Air Support Group engaged in operations for the capture of the Japanese-held Southern Marianas Islands during the period 14 June to 1 August 1944. By his understanding initiative, and outstanding ability, he conducted well-coordinated bombing and strafing missions, antisubmarine and combat air patrols in support of the amphibious landings in this theater. His escort carriers were well organized and excellently handled their many aggressive missions contributed materially to the success of the operations . . ."

Navy Cross: "For extraordinary heroism as Commander Task Group 38.2, during operations against enemy Japanese forces, November 25, 1944. When all the carriers under his command were damaged by enemy aerial attack, including two bomb hits on his own Flagship, Rear Admiral Bogan continued to fight his forces so vigorously that eight enemy aircraft were shot down by his ship's gunfire, and the remaining enemy aircraft driven away. By his courage and leadership, he contributed directly to the success of our forces in this area . . ."

Distinguished Service Medal: "For exceptionally meritorious service to the Government in a duty of great responsibility while serving as Commander of a Task Group assigned to duty with the Second Carrier Task Force, Pacific Fleet, from 30 October 1944 to 25 January 1945. Under his direction his Task Group completed highly successful operations against enemy aircraft, shipping and land installations in the Philippine Islands, Formosa, the Nansei Shoto Islands and the Coast of Indo-China. His ability to organize, direct and inspire the forces under his command to their maximum effort resulted in devastating damage being inflicted on the enemy . . ."

Gold star in lieu of second Distinguished Service Medal: ". . . As Commander Task Group 38.3, from July 1 to September 2, 1945 . . . Rear Admiral Bogan pressed home devastating attacks on the home land of Japan in coordination with other task groups, directing destructive strikes against aircraft and supporting industries, installations and transportation facilities and concentrations of naval vessels at Yokosuka, Kure and Kobe. Under repeated aerial attacks delivered by the desperate Japanese, he maintained a high standard of fighting efficiency in all his gallant ships and employed brilliant defensive tactics in repulsing the fanatic enemy. [His] fearless leadership and his expert tactical control of the carriers, battleships, cruisers and destroyers in Task Group 38.3 were vital factors in the infliction of extensive damage on the enemy and in the completion of hazardous missions without damage to his own ships . . ."

In September 1945, following the capitulation of the Japanese the preceding August, Admiral Bogan returned to the United States and in October assumed command of Fleet Air, Alameda, California. On 2 February 1946 he became Commander Air Force, Atlantic Fleet, with the accompanying rank of vice admiral. Orders of July 1948 relieved him of that command and designated him Commander First Task Fleet. He assumed command on 8 January 1949, and remained in that command until his retirement became effective on 1 February 1950.

In addition to the Navy Cross, Distinguished Service Medal with Gold Star, the Legion of Merit, Vice Admiral Bogan held the Presidential Unit Citation with four stars; the Navy Expeditionary Medal (Siberia, 1922); the Victory Medal, Escort Clasp; the American Defense Service Medal, Fleet Clasp; Asiatic-Pacific Campaign Medal with operation stars; American Campaign Medal; World War II Victory Medal; and Philippine Liberation Ribbon, with one star.

Admiral Bogan died on 8 June 1973 at La Jolla, California.

Interview Number 1 with Vice Admiral Gerald F. Bogan,
U.S. Navy (Retired)

Place: Admiral Bogan's home in La Jolla, California

Date: 25 December 1969

Subject: Biography

Interviewer: Commander Etta-Belle Kitchen, U.S. Navy (Retired)

Q: Admiral Bogan, the Institute is extremely pleased that you will take the time to give us your recollections and to make alive some of those words that are in the history books about you.

Admiral Bogan: Time is what I have the most of.

Q: Well, that's just wonderful. If you have any introductory comments, I'd be glad to have them; otherwise, we might as well start at the beginning of your career.

Admiral Bogan: Let's go.

Q: Tell me how you happened to select the Navy.

Admiral Bogan: I suppose it was a premature decision, but when I was five years old, my father, who was a doctor, took a short postgraduate course at the Polyclinic Hospital in New York City.

My mother and I went with him, and during the course of his two months' stay there we visited the Brooklyn Navy Yard.* It was shortly after the end of the Spanish-American War, and I went aboard these various battleships which had participated in the Battle of Santiago, and at that time I told him that I wanted to go to the Naval Academy and join the Navy.** Our home was in Mackinac Island, Michigan. I lived only a few hundred feet from the water, and eventually I went to the Naval Academy.

Q: Were you appointed by a local congressman, or how did you get into the Academy?

Admiral Bogan: I learned my first lesson in politics through trying to enter the Naval Academy. My father, being a doctor, had no political influence and I received an alternate appointment and took the mental examinations which I passed. But my principal succeeded in entering, so I was left out for that year. I was going to school in Chicago at the time, and I found out from the congressman of the district in which I lived that he had two appointments for the Naval Academy. He was reluctant to appoint me, but through a distant relative who had had a great deal to do with his election, he gave me the appointment, only to

---
*The official name for the yard was New York Navy Yard.
**The battle off Santiago, Cuba, on 3 July 1898 resulted in a U.S. victory over a force of Spanish cruisers.

tell me two days later that he could not do it because I was not a resident of Chicago, but a resident of Michigan. So I went to my relative again, who called the congressman on the telephone and said, "Listen, Mr. Evans, when I got you elected I promised not to ask any favors from you, and I'm not doing it now. I'm just telling you, appoint this young man."* And I was appointed.

Q: It's a singular thing, Admiral, that as I observe men who have been tremendously successful in the Navy, invariably something in the nature of your experience happened, in that they weren't the first ones selected, or they were an alternate and something happened that, through a series of events, they got into the Navy, which I think is kind of interesting.

Admiral Bogan: It gave me a lesson in politics, and later I had a firsthand lesson in Communism in Siberia.

Q: We're going to talk about that, I hope. I'm going to make a note of that so we won't forget it.
I know that you were interested in sports while you were in the Academy. Can you tell me your recollections of it, and whether you enjoyed it?

---

*Representative Lynden Evans, Democrat of Chicago, in Illinois's ninth district.

Bogan #1 - 4

Admiral Bogan: I enjoyed it greatly. I weighed about 160 pounds then, and 165 now. I played on the class football team for four years, and I went out for crew for four years. In spite of my lack of height, I did get the letter N in my first-class year for winning a race, being a member of the crew that won the Henley race in Philadelphia. That, I guess, was probably my athletic activity at the Naval Academy.

Q: Do you have any recollections or anecdotes that you would like to relate?

Admiral Bogan: If you're not on the first team, it's just plugging to try to get recognition all the time. I was what you might call on B squad in football, and second and third crew until my last year, when I finally was selected in a four-oared crew and we won the Henley race.

Q: That's good enough. Who was it said, "There's first place and all the rest"?

Admiral Bogan: That's right.

Q: As you look back, do you think your experience at the Academy fitted you for your later career in the Navy?

Admiral Bogan: It was a largely technical education, and in thinking of it later, I thought that the one benefit that I got out of it was that it did teach me how to study, because I learned more after I got out of the Academy than I ever learned there, except the discipline, which you learned quickly or you weren't there very long. I believe that the Academy has greatly improved in the last 25 years.

Q: I was going to ask you what your feeling of the Academy . . .

Admiral Bogan: Of course, I'm not close to it, but they've broadened the faculty members. When I was there, two-thirds of the instructors were naval officers who regarded two years at the Naval Academy as a nice rest period, and we never got any real instruction. We'd have a lesson assignment; we'd come to class in groups or sections of 12 or 14, and the instructor would say, "draw slips," and we'd answer the questions on the board and he'd mark us. There was no real instruction. I thought it would have been of greater benefit to the students had there been instruction. When I was later assigned for one year as an instructor at the Academy, I had the first 20 minutes of discussion of the lesson, and 20 minutes recitation, and the last 20 minutes trying to answer questions which the section would give me. I hope that was of more benefit to them than the kind of instruction I received seven years earlier.

Bogan #1 - 6

Q: You applied what you felt was a lack when you had the opportunity.

Admiral Bogan: I tried to do it, yes.

Q: Do you remember any anecdotes about some of the people who were with you at the Academy in those days?

Admiral Bogan: There was a man named I.C. Kidd--his son, by the way, has just taken command of the First Fleet--and he was a real love child, although we didn't call him a love child.* He was in the discipline department, and the midshipmen's nickname for him was "I Catch 'em Kidd" because he was like an Indian scout, hiding behind places and trying to nab midshipmen breaking the rules and regulations, which he often succeeded in doing. I've never been able to understand why, when he was killed in the Arizona at Pearl Harbor, he was later given a posthumous Medal of Honor, because there was nothing that he could have done in the Arizona that would warrant any award, particularly of that degree. But, aside from him, I don't remember many of the instructors.

---
*Lieutenant Isaac C. Kidd, USN. His son, Isaac C. Kidd, Jr., eventually retired from active duty in 1978 as a four-star admiral.

Bogan #1 - 7

Q: I meant your classmates.

Admiral Bogan: I had a few close friends, but--no, I don't think I could offer anything.

Q: Many of the men who became heroes, famous, well-known in World War II were all people whom you knew, of course.

Admiral Bogan: Oh, yes.

Q: From Academy days?

Admiral Bogan: Berkey was a classmate of mine.* Wheeler, whom we've mentioned.** Moon, who was a very brilliant man, suicided shortly after the Normandy invasion.*** But, aside from Berkey, none of the three people I've mentioned were close associates. Berkey and I were in the same company for three years.

Q: The Navy was small enough in those days that you knew most everyone in it, didn't you?

---
*Midshipman Russell S. Berkey, who reached three-star rank by the time of his retirement in 1950.
**Midshipman Charles J. Wheeler, who was a captain at the time of his retirement in 1948. Wheeler's oral history is in the Naval Institute's collection.
***Rear Admiral Don P. Moon, USN, killed himself on 5 August 1944.

Bogan #1 - 8

Admiral Bogan: There were only 800 men at the Academy when I was a midshipman, and we graduated 177 out of the class that entered of 278.

Q: That's fair attrition, isn't it?

Admiral Bogan: Better than 30%.

Q: Yes. Where were you in your class?

Admiral Bogan: I was 24 or 25, I think.*

Q: That's very good.

Admiral Bogan: It's in the upper half, anyway.

Q: Yes, indeed. What is your next recollection? I indicate that after graduation you went to a battleship.

Admiral Bogan: I went to the Vermont for four months. She was decommissioned in October. Then until the beginning of World War I, under Secretary Daniels's educational program, I taught recruits the third grade at the naval station at Great Lakes

---

*Bogan stood number 26 of 177 in the class of 1916.

Training Station, and if you don't think that was a difficult job, you're wrong.*

Q: Tell me about that.

Admiral Bogan: These great big Iowa farmers would come in the Navy to get away from farming, and here they were sent to school for two hours a day at Great Lakes in addition to their drill.

Q: You taught them what, did you say?

Admiral Bogan: I was teaching the third grade, the equivalent of third grade in grammar school.

Q: Not really.

Admiral Bogan: Actually.

Q: These were the recruits?

Admiral Bogan: These were the recruits.

Q: Had they had no education at all?

---
*Josephus Daniels was Secretary of the Navy from 1913 to 1921.

Admiral Bogan: Apparently not, because we'd grade them when they'd come in and assign them to the various--I don't think there were any grades higher than five that they were taking. But they were big, strong, willing boys, except where book learning was concerned.

Then, at the beginning of World War I, the day after war was declared, I was ordered to the Birmingham.* She was an overgrown destroyer. They called her a light cruiser. We ran antisubmarine patrols off the Atlantic coast, between Martha's Vineyard and New York, for two months, then took the first convoy to France, landing at St. Nazaire on the third or fourth of July.

Q: Did you go clear in to France?

Admiral Bogan: Yes, we landed. We went in to St. Nazaire, and although we had no submarine contacts on the way over, the evidence of the submarine campaign was clearly evident, because the last 300 miles off the coast of France was filled with wreckage, dead bodies, swamped boats--lifeboats--and cargo from these ships. Then we were ordered to Gibraltar, and from that time until the end of the war we ran convoy between Great Britain and Gibraltar, escorting over 500 ships without the loss of a single ship.

---
*The United States entered World War I on 6 April 1917, the date of the congressional declaration of war.

Bogan #1 - 11

Q: This was escorting British ships or American ships?

Admiral Bogan: Merchant ships, any nation.

Q: I see.

Admiral Bogan: The convoys would come out of the Mediterranean and re-form at Gibraltar and be assembled. Then we'd take them up, sometimes to Milford Haven in Wales or as far as Plymouth in the English Channel. And the same thing on the way back. We'd meet a convoy and take it to Gibraltar.

Q: How many days would you be at sea? You didn't touch shore either time?

Admiral Bogan: We entered port for bunker coal at each end. All these convoys were called seven-knot convoys, but invariably there would be one ship in the group which would make five knots, and that was the speed we'd make. It took us anywhere from nine to 12 days to make the 1,000 miles, or 1,100 miles, from Gibraltar to England. An express convoy, which we'd get occasionally, was listed at ten knots, and they were ships that were capable of making 15 or 16 and, in that case, the trip would take about six days.

Bogan #1 - 12

Q: Did you have submarine contact frequently, or not?

Admiral Bogan: We never saw a submarine.

Q: You never saw one? You said you didn't lose a ship, but I didn't know whether you saw any submarines or not.

Admiral Bogan: One night there was an amusing thing. Just after dark, a submarine was reported on the surface, and I ran aft to my battery and turned the searchlight on and saw it was a dead whale. In the meantime, the captain was on the bridge yelling, "Fire, for Christ's sake, fire." I told him over the telephone it was a whale, and it was a fortunate thing that we did not fire because one of the gun's crew had forgotten to take the tampion out of the muzzle of the gun. Had we fired with that thing in there, the gun would have blown up and probably everybody around it.

Q: That's right. I'm awfully glad you thought to look. What job did you have on this ship?

Admiral Bogan: I was a division officer, and, for a while, the gunnery officer. But the battery was very small. We had 4- or 5-inch guns.

Q: Was this when you were on the Stribling?

Admiral Bogan: No. At the end of the war, as the bells for the armistice were tolling, and everybody was preparing for a massive drunk, we sailed from Gibraltar for Venice, to be flagship of Admiral Bullard, and a new setup in the Adriatic Sea.* After two months of that duty, the Birmingham was ordered back and I was able to prevail on the skipper to allow me to transfer to a destroyer which was there, the Stribling, which needed an officer. I spent the next nine months in her and returned to the United States in the late summer of 1919.

Q: Did you enjoy that duty?

Admiral Bogan: Very much. The Adriatic's is the most wonderful scenery in the world, particularly on the eastern side where we were.

Q: The Dalmatian coast?

Admiral Bogan: Yes, all the way down from Trieste right down to Cattaro, which is now called Kotor, and the Bay of Cattaro is unbelievable when you go into it.

---

*Rear Admiral William H.G. Bullard, USN, commanding naval forces operating in the Eastern Mediterranean.

Q: I don't know the Bay of Cattaro.

Admiral Bogan: It used to be--the Italian name for it was Cattaro, and near there is Dubrovnik, which used to be called Ragusa.

Q: Do you remember any particular anecdotes from those days?

Admiral Bogan: We were based a great part of the time at Spalato, which is now called Split, and Admiral Phillip Andrews had his flagship, the old Olympia, there.* Diocletian's Palace, the old Roman emperor's palace, is still there, or the ruins of it.** Every time any Americans went ashore, we were followed by crowds of kids yelling, "Dobre Americani, tchokalati, tchokalati." Admiral Andrews usually took a pocketful of chocolates with him, so he was called, "Dobre Americani, dobre almirante."

Q: What does that mean?

Admiral Bogan: Dobre--good admiral.

---
*Rear Admiral Phillip Andrews, USN, commanding naval forces operating in the Eastern Mediterranean.
**Diocletian was Roman Emperor from 284 to 305. His name came from his birth at Dioclea in Dalmatia.

Q: What was your job on the ship, then, Admiral?

Admiral Bogan: We had two reserves and a captain and, when I reported aboard, an executive officer and a gunnery officer. I was to relieve the gunnery officer, who immediately went ashore with a split appendix. The executive officer was ordered back to command a new destroyer, so after six weeks, I had every job on the ship except captain.

Q: Is that right?

Admiral Bogan: It really wasn't long enough. It was a great experience, it was interesting, and gave me a sense of responsibility, and I enjoyed it. I enjoyed all of it.

Q: You were just a youngster then, too, actually in years?

Admiral Bogan: I was 24.

Q: You didn't think you were a youngster at that time, I'm sure.

Admiral Bogan: Oh, no, of course not. Just as I don't think I'm an old man now, when I know I am.

Q: Oh, I don't think you are.

Bogan #1 - 16

Admiral Bogan: I'm 75.

Q: To me, age--I hope--isn't a matter of calendar years.

Admiral Bogan: No, it isn't.

Q: I was interested in what you said about wanting to live in a community where there were diverse interests, rather than an ingrown group. Do you want to expand on that? I'd love to hear your philosophy.

Admiral Bogan: I believe that the first and most serious sign of aging is getting thick between the ears, and if you live in a closed community, such as Coronado, where 50% are retired military, there is not the incentive to keep alive, to keep on your toes, as there are in other places.

Q: There isn't the diverse interest, is what you mean.

Admiral Bogan: That's what I mean.

Q: Do you want to contribute with any other anecdotes about your experience in the <u>Stribling</u>?

Admiral Bogan: Yes.

Bogan #1 - 17

Q: And the Hopewell and the Broome, successively?

Admiral Bogan: That's right. We came back to the United States in the summer of '19. The ship was ordered to Portsmouth (New Hampshire) Navy Yard for an overhaul, and half of the crew was detached. We were practically in reserve and I saw no means of getting out of there, so I wrote to Abel Bidwell, who had been my exec in the Birmingham and was then in the Bureau of Navigation, and asked if he could get me an active destroyer.* So I was ordered as chief engineer of the Hopewell. This was just after the war, when the ships used to go up rivers and recruit bums from the wharf and put them aboard and put a uniform on them. The situation was grim.

Q: Were those the days where people were told, "If you don't want to go to jail, you can go in the Navy"?

Admiral Bogan: Yes.

Q: So you got aboard the Hopewell.

Admiral Bogan: Went in the Hopewell, and we were down on a training cruise at Guantanamo and Guacanayabo Gulf in Cuba for

---
*Lieutenant Commander Abel T. Bidwell, USN.

four months. At the end of that time, I was able to be assigned as executive officer to the Broome, which was going back to Europe, where I wanted to go. We spent the summer of 1920 in Europe and the Baltic down through the Mediterranean, and in January of '21, the division was ordered to the Philippines. We went out in two sections of three boats each and arrived in the Philippines at the end of January.

The following January, when the Broome was due to come home, I was ordered to take command of a naval radio station on Russian Island, which is across the entrance to the harbor from Vladivostok.

Q: I was interested in that.

Admiral Bogan: The genesis of our being there is somewhat odd, but in 1918, after the Russian Revolution, the Russians themselves were starting to build on Russian Island a duplicate of a large radio station in Moscow. The Japanese had quite an army in the Allied force in Siberia at that time, and the United States station ship sent 20 Marines over to take possession of this embryo station before the Japs got it. They were two hours ahead of 200 Japs. We concluded an agreement with the then-governor of the Far Eastern Republic, which consisted of the five maritime provinces on the Pacific northeast of Russia--which were then not overrun by the Bolsheviks--that we would construct this station. At the beginning of the first stable Russian government, we would return the station to the Russian stable government with its existing equipment. I arrived there in January of 1922, and in October of that year . . .

Q: You were the commanding officer, weren't you?

Admiral Bogan: I was the commanding officer, yes. I had a warrant officer, 20 Marines, and 35 Navy enlisted men.

Q: Can you describe it before you go on?

Admiral Bogan: It was an unpretentious looking thing, but it was the main link in all the communications from the Commander in Chief Asiatic to the United States. A large station had been in the process of construction at Peking for that purpose, but while they were testing the boilers they burnt them up, leaving Russian Island as the only connecting link. And, being as far north as it was, the atmospheric conditions for transmission were far more stable in that area than farther south, which made it an ideal place. We used to relay to St. Paul on Pribilof Island, to Guam, and on occasion to Honolulu. But all the Asiatic traffic was cleared through that station.

Q: From our fleet?

Admiral Bogan: Yes, from our fleet, and some diplomatic came through there. In October, when the Communists came in, after the Japs had pulled out . . .

Q: Excuse me, the Japs weren't there when you were, were they?

Admiral Bogan: The Japs were in Siberia. They were stretched up as far as Lake Baikal, Irkutsk, 1,500 miles inland. When the Paris Peace Conference in the summer of '22 indicated that they had better get out, the Bolsheviks came down behind them and took over what was then called the Far Eastern Republic.

Q: How did the U.S. Navy get involved in this radio station?

Admiral Bogan: As I explained--or thought I explained--earlier, we had taken it to keep the Japs from getting it.

Q: Did we go in as a military operation?

Admiral Bogan: Yes. It was a naval radio station, and we sent our equipment and made an operating unit out of it. The main power plant was a 250-horsepower diesel engine that had been used in a mine in Montana, and the secondary one had been used in a radio station at Hilo. It was primitive, the equipment, but we had arc transmitters, and it was very efficient for its day and age.

When the Bolsheviks took Vladivostok, they found this agreement saying we would turn it over to the first stable Russian government, and they went to the commanding officer of the station ship and said, "We are the stable government. When will you get out of Russian Island?"

Q: That was you?

Admiral Bogan: That was me. So the Commander in Chief Asiatic sent the <u>Pecos</u>, a tanker, up to Vladivostok to take our personnel. We did not leave the most advanced equipment we had, but we left them a working station, and I came down to Manila in December of '22.

Q: Did you clear with the U.S. Government or the head of the fleet that this was a stable government? Did you get permission to turn it over?

Admiral Bogan: There was an American consul there. It was all done through him.

Q: I see.

Admiral Bogan: And there was this agreement we would turn over

Bogan #1 - 22

to the first stable government; there was no other government. If they wanted to claim, that was it. What could we do? We had one gunboat there and Russian Island, which had 20 Marines.

Q: But I wondered if you made the decision yourself.

Admiral Bogan: I had nothing to do with making the decision.

Q: You said to me a minute ago that you learned about Communism, too, in Siberia. Was this the incident?

Admiral Bogan: No, this was not the incident. Before the Communists had come in, there was a Russian officer in the militia on Russian Island who used to come and visit me frequently. I'd feed him well and see that he got enough vodka to go off pleased. When the last six men and myself were to go to Vladivostok to board the station ship for transportation to Manila, I had rented a little boat to take us across the five miles, and there were about 25 civilians who wanted to take that boat. I said, no, I'd paid for it, it's my boat. They said, "But we're the public." So I quoted Commodore Vanderbilt and said, "Chort s'publikami," which means in Russian, "To hell with the public."*

One of them disappeared, and in a few minutes after that, my friend whom I'd entertained so often came down and said, "Because you have been good to me and because you have never experienced or voiced opposition to me, I will tell you now that I was the advanced agent of the Communist government all the time I was visiting you, and because you are my friend, you were permitted to take this boat and go across." That was in a nutshell the basis of Communism today. They respect only one thing--power. If they think they're stronger, they will do anything until they run up against what they consider is an impossible block, and only then. And, to me, this business of trying to seek better relations with the Russians, or anyone else in the Communist Empire, is the height of idiocy. They are committed to world domination under a Communist form of government until internal conditions in their own country render that impossible. We are living on the edge of a precipice.

Q: They're not going to change until some force . . .

---

*In 1889, railroad tycoon William H. Vanderbilt was asked whether it was in the public interest to remove a fast daily train between New York and Chicago. His reported answer, which has since been widely quoted, "The public be damned. We don't take any stock in this silly nonsense working for anybody's good but our own--because we are not."

Admiral Bogan: Greater than their own government and probably internally makes it possible for them to be overturned. This Czechoslovakian thing is the most recent example.*

Q: Did you recognize in the days when you were dealing with the Russians, that would have been in 1922, that this was their feeling?

Admiral Bogan: Until the Communists took over in October [1917], most of the people there were refugees from the Communist revolution in western Russia, and the average Russian is very similar to the United States citizen in his hospitality and his generosity. They are much more generous than we are. They're a trusting people, and they would like to live in peace. That is the average Russian. The average Russian today, even under Communism, is dominated by a government that allows him no freedom.

Q: Let's go back and talk about when you were in the <u>Broome</u> in the Baltic.

---

*In July 1968, just over a year before this interview was conducted, Soviet, Polish, East German, Hungarian, and Bulgarian military forces invaded Czechoslovakia to put an end to a liberalization movement which had taken hold in the Communist-dominated country.

Admiral Bogan: We were in the Baltic as tender to the Pittsburgh for two months in the fall of '20, and we were in Riga for ten days at a time when the Polish-Russian War was concluded. The reason it was concluded in a hurry was that General Wrangel was making great inroads against the Red Russian armies with his White Army.* So the Russian delegates and the Polish delegates assembled at Riga, and I was amazed because members of the proletariat arrived in a great big procession of fine cars with fat Jewish women having jewels all up their arms, which they'd probably stolen from somebody else. And the peace treaty was concluded.

Q: Did you say "Jewish women"?

Admiral Bogan: Oh, yes. A lot of the original Red Russkies were Jewish. Trotsky was a Jew.** His name was Bronstein, and others--he had a great many of them. Beria was a Jew.*** But, anyway, that peace treaty allowed the Russians to send Budenny's

---

*Baron Petr Nikolaevich Wrangel, a Russian general who had served in the Russo-Japanese War and World War I. In April 1920 he was appointed commander in chief as a volunteer anti-Bolshevik army. After initial successes, his forces lost Sevastopol in November 1920, and he and his troops evacuated to Yugoslavia.
**Leon Trotsky, an early Bolshevik leader, whose real name was Leib Davydovich Bronstein.
***Lavrenti Pavlovich Beria, chief of the public security organization in the Caucasus from 1921 to 1931.

army down to fight Wrangel.* And instead of having to go around these marshes, which would ordinarily be necessary, to fight Wrangel, a very cold spell froze them and he was able to walk over to defeat him.

From there we went around to Constantinople and helped evacuate the parts of Wrangel's army to a refugee camp on the Bay of Cattaro in the Adriatic, and from there we went on out to the Philippines.

Q: Was that interesting?

Admiral Bogan: Oh, it was very interesting. We docked at Odessa to take a load of refugees, some of whom we dropped at Constantinople, some at Prinkipo Island in the Sea of Marmara, and the rest at a refugee camp off the Adriatic.

Q: You said there was a girl on the dock that wanted to go.

Admiral Bogan: At Odessa, and because we already had a load, including many on deck, I said no more could come. She said, through her tears, "Bolsheviks came, they shot my mother, they shot my father, and they screwed me."

---

*Semen Mikhailovich Budenny, a Russian soldier who had entered the army in 1903 and served as a cavalry leader in the campaign against Wrangel.

Q: Oh, I thought they shot her. But you couldn't take her aboard?

Admiral Bogan: Oh, I took her, sure.

Q: I'm glad. What was one more!

Admiral Bogan: No, it didn't make any difference, really, but we thought we had a safe load, all we could squeeze on deck.

Q: You know, sometimes you say a thing that happened and then when you go back and describe some of the personal incidents that happened, it makes a story that isn't apparent just from the comment.
   Did we finish with the radio station up on Russian Island?

Admiral Bogan: Yes.

Q: Then, you said, you went down to Manila?

Admiral Bogan: Down to Manila, and came back to the United States in a transport. I had been trying for several years to be assigned to aviation duty, but it was not the policy to order anyone from abroad home for aviation duty.

Q: Why not?

Admiral Bogan: Ask them. And instead of going to Pensacola, I was ordered to the Naval Academy to take the place of a man named Rosendahl, who had just been assigned to lighter-than-air training.* At the end of a year, the Superintendent requested my detachment from the Naval Academy because he gave me credit for making a home run when I hadn't even got to first base.

Q: What do you mean?

Admiral Bogan: Taking this girl around. She was married, and I was taking her around, but I hadn't had any success. However, he credited me with success I hadn't had.

From there I was ordered to Pensacola.

Q: I think it might be interesting on your experience in Annapolis--this is when you said, on returning, you tried to teach the way you thought teaching should be. Can you amplify on that a little bit?

Admiral Bogan: I'd rather not. I mean, it's not important.

---

*Lieutenant Charles E. Rosendahl, USN.

Bogan #1 - 29

Q: Okay. So, anyway, then where did you go from the Academy?

Admiral Bogan: I went to the naval air station at Pensacola as a student aviator.

Q: Did you go by way of Hampton Roads, Virginia?

Admiral Bogan: I was on orders to temporary duty at Hampton Roads, Virginia, until the beginning of the next class of students at Pensacola, which took place in July of '24.

Q: A friend of mine, Admiral Van Deurs, thought he gave you your first ride in an airplane.* Is that true?

Admiral Bogan: That's not true. My first ride in an airplane was given to me by Admiral Mitscher when I was on my way to the Naval Academy in '23.** I went over to the naval air station at Anacostia and he was about to take off in an experimental plane and I asked him for a ride.

Q: That was your first experience?

---
*Ensign George Van Deurs, USN. His oral history is in the Naval Institute collection.
**Lieutenant Commander Marc A. Mitscher, USN, later noted as a carrier task force commander in World War II.

Bogan #1 - 30

Admiral Bogan: That was my first.

Q: Admiral Van Deurs said that he took you from Norfolk up to the Academy, while you were stationed in Norfolk.

Admiral Bogan: At that time?

Q: Yes.

Admiral Bogan: Could be. I've forgotten.

Q: It was a memorable experience for him. He remembered that very well. Then tell me about Pensacola.

Admiral Bogan: Pensacola, I thought then--of course, it's been immeasurably improved now--had a very fine course of instruction. When we got our wings 11 months later, we had about 250 hours in the air in all types of planes from the old primary training seaplane to the big boats and a few of the planes which were then being used in the operating squadrons. While our education was sketchy, I think it was basically sound.

Q: Any land planes?

Admiral Bogan: Yes, both land planes and seaplanes. The first half of the course was in seaplanes, and the second half was in land planes.

Q: Any carrier training?

Admiral Bogan: Not then. The Langley was the only carrier at that time, and one squadron was qualified on the West Coast. When I arrived at the West Coast, the squadron to which I was ordered had been put on floats and was operating from battleships on that cruise. When they came back, we went on wheels again, and a few months later qualified on the Langley as a squadron. We were attached to the Langley from the middle of '25 until '28. I had reported as executive officer to the squadron and had command of it for the last two years.

Q: That was going into command pretty quickly, wasn't it?

Admiral Bogan: Not too quickly.

Q: I'd love to have you repeat that, the fact that you were 30 when you went to flight training, and you were older than the other men in the class.

Admiral Bogan: The Navy policy at that time was to order a graduating class to at least two years of sea duty before being

Bogan #1 - 32

assigned to aviation duty. As a result of that policy, I, who had graduated in 1916 and was eight years out of the Naval Academy, was several years older than most of my classmates.

Q: You were 30 then?

Admiral Bogan: I was 30, and I felt that I had to perhaps try a little harder to show them that a decrepit old man could do the same things they did as well or better.

Q: I suppose, really, to them, 30 seemed pretty old, didn't it?

Admiral Bogan: Certainly.

Q: Who were some of your classmates there at Pensacola?

Admiral Bogan: That great naval hero, Jock Clark, was one.* Lawrence Richardson, who was an aeronautical engineering duty only, was almost as old as I; he was another.** He died in July 1969.

Q: I think Admiral Stroop said you were the squadron commander

---
*Lieutenant Joseph J. Clark, USN, who became a carrier task group commander in World War II.
**Lieutenant Lawrence B. Richardson, Construction Corps, USN.

when he took flight training.*

Q: That's right, but on a later tour at Pensacola.

Admiral Bogan: And you felt the training was satisfying to you. Why had you wanted to become an aviator?

Admiral Bogan: I knew that if I had to do much battleship duty, I'd get out of the Navy, because to me it's a very uninteresting, very dull, and step-by-step regulation. Next to that, destroyer duty was fine, and I had four years of that--every job from chief engineer to skipper for a temporary time. But aviation, to me, has always been what I thought was the wave of the future as far as the Navy was concerned, where you're responsible for everything you do, you pay for your mistakes, and, conversely, you hope to be rewarded for good work. And that's why I wanted to go in aviation.

Q: Do you like to fly?

Admiral Bogan: Very much, always.

---

*Vice Admiral Paul D. Stroop, USN(Ret.), whose oral history is in the Naval Institute collection.

Bogan #1 - 34

Q: Do you have any more comments about Pensacola?

Admiral Bogan: No, I don't.

Q: Then your next duty was--you spoke briefly of the Langley. Can you amplify some of your experiences on it?

Admiral Bogan: I was in VF Squadron One, at that time, and, as I say, I was executive officer the first year, and moved up to skipper for the following two years. We participated in all the fleet cruises, and about that time Commodore J.M. Reeves became Commander Aircraft Battle Force.* I believe that although he had no background in aviation that it was his intention and driving ambition to make aviation an integral part of the fleet. That changed it from a group of squadrons acting independently, and at times to each other's disadvantage, into a cohesive whole which later became Naval Air Force Pacific Fleet and was a complete entity.

As I say, he did not have much of an aviation background, and, as an instance of this, on one occasion in the summer of '27, we were on our way from San Diego to Seattle in the Langley,

---
*In 1925, after qualifying at Pensacola as a naval aviation observer, Captain Joseph M. Reeves, USN, hoisted his broad pennant in the carrier Langley (CV-1), and thus was entitled to be addressed as commodore. In 1927, he was promoted to rear admiral, and the title of his billet was later upgraded to Commander Carriers Battle Fleet.

when Commodore Reeves decided that the time had come to break the record for carrier landings made in a single day. He sent for me and for Commander Mitscher, who was then air officer of the Langley, and said this was a good time to do it. I explained to him that the wind was blowing 50 knots, that the planes landed at about 52. The Langley needed at least eight knots for steerageway, and that she was pitching 24 or 30 feet.* I said it was going to be very difficult to land into the sea and wind conditions as they were. Commodore Reeves said, "Not at all. We'll just steam downwind." I thought Pete Mitscher was going to vomit, but he didn't, and we began the landings under those conditions. We did break the record, and then two or three of my pilots refused to fly, so I took one of their planes in the morning and took my own in the afternoon. Later that afternoon, toward the end of the day, my tailhook caught a fore-and-aft wire, and I went over the side and was picked up by the Aroostook, which was plane tending.

Q: Were you in the plane, or did you lose the plane?

Admiral Bogan: When they threw me a line from the Aroostook, I tried to get it around the tail of the plane, but she sank as I reached for it, so I tied it around myself and they hauled me up

---

*Steerageway is the slowest speed at which a ship can be steered.

to the deck.

Q: I wouldn't really care whether they got the plane or not, as long as they got you.

Admiral Bogan: They did.

Q: That area going up toward Seattle, is horrible; it has lots of terrible, bad weather.

Admiral Bogan: It can be good or bad; there's no middle ground. It's not moderate. It's either good or bad.

Q: But you did break the record?

Admiral Bogan: I think we made 129 landings.

Q: That's so unimportant, isn't it?

Admiral Bogan: It had absolutely no significance. He just wanted to break a record, and we did it under very adverse conditions. But it is unimportant.

Q: I would think so. After all, you're not out there to play games.

Bogan #1 - 37

Admiral Bogan: That's right.

Q: You only lost one plane. I'm surprised they didn't lose more than one.

Admiral Bogan: We broke a couple of wheels.

Q: What did he think when he saw the dangerous situation he'd created?

Admiral Bogan: He didn't think. He didn't know enough about it.

Q: Even after it was going on, didn't he realize it was dangerous?

Admiral Bogan: No, because he was a very determined man and a brilliant man, but he just had a blind spot there. We were going to break the record, period. On the way back from Seattle, the Secretary of the Navy was in one of the battleships. Reeves called me in and said, "Now, I want you to give a good demonstration over the California for Secretary Wilbur."*

I said, "Commodore, there's a storm coming in here from the

---
*Curtis D. Wilbur, Secretary of the Navy from March 1924 to March 1929. The USS California (BB-44) was flagship of the Battle Fleet.

northwest."

"Oh, it amounts to nothing." So we went off, and we hadn't been in the air 15 minutes before this thing hit, and if conditions on the record-setting day were bad, these were worse because the rain was driving down in such sheets that you could barely see the deck. We got away with it. Not a wheel was broken and not a tire blown.

Q: Again, it seems to me, a demonstration for no particular purpose.

Admiral Bogan: That's right. And in reviewing this little cruise at a critique at North Island a few weeks later, he said, "Gentlemen, you went to Seattle neophytes, and you came back veterans."

I said, "Yes, and we were lucky to come back."

Q: Good for you. This is an incident, it seems to me, which shows the mistake of putting a non-aviator in charge of a carrier.

Admiral Bogan: But, you see, he was not in charge of the carrier. He was in command of all the aircraft of the Pacific Fleet. Langley was his flagship. What they had done, and it was necessary at that time--most of the aviators were very junior;

they didn't have the rank to command a carrier. They sent a number of senior officers, commanders, to Pensacola and one or two of them actually completed the course. As a matter of fact, Admiral Halsey at 51 did successfully complete the course.*

Admiral Bogan: Didn't Admiral King, too?

Admiral Bogan: Admiral King did, too, but Admiral King--yes, he completed the course.**

Q: You were going to say something and decided not to.

Admiral Bogan: Well, Admiral King was a man who always flew an aircraft into a landing faster than it needed to go, and on occasion he ran out of field at the end of his landing. That's what I was going to say.

Q: Well, fortunately for us, he didn't crack himself up.

Admiral Bogan: Ah, he was a great guy.

---

*Captain William F. Halsey, Jr., entered flight training in July 1934 and was designated a naval aviator in May 1935 at the age of 52. As an admiral in World War II, he was Commander Third Fleet.
**Captain Ernest J. King, USN, got his aviator's wings in 1927 at age 48. He was Chief of Naval Operations and Commander in Chief U.S. Fleet in World War II.

Q: You told Admiral Reeves you were lucky to get back.

Admiral Bogan: After this trip to Seattle, then I was ordered in 1928 to Pensacola for two years as instructor and commanding officer of the primary training squadron. And after the first year of that, I became a chief check pilot down there, to corroborate or disagree with the previous check pilots who failed a man. It was my decision whether he'd get three more hours extra time or be forced out. In 1930 I came back and took VF-3, which was another fighting squadron, and we were attached to the Lexington.

Q: When you were at Pensacola on this job, did you ever give anyone an opportunity to take the additional hours that you later regretted?

Admiral Bogan: No, I don't think so, because if three hours wouldn't do it, they failed the next check and they would automatically go out.

Q: Then you came back to join the fighting squadron on the . . .

Admiral Bogan: In the Lexington. I spent one year there. The Langley, at that time, had an enlisted men's squadron aboard, and

Dave Ingalls, who was Assistant Secretary of the Navy for Air, thought that she ought to have a squadron composed of commissioned officers, because she was being transferred to the East Coast, and the squadron would participate in a good many of the air shows that were prevalent at that time.*

Q: That was unusual to have a squadron of enlisted men, wasn't it?

Admiral Bogan: VF-2 was composed as an enlisted squadron. The six section leaders were officers, and the two other pilots in each section were enlisted men, and some of them were some of the best pilots in the Navy. I have a very good friend over here in Harry Holt, who retired as a commander, who was in that squadron for a good many years.** I've never known a finer man nor a finer pilot. A great many of them are dead now. A few are retired in Coronado, but it was a fine squadron. Anyway, we replaced them in the Langley, and flew from Pensacola to Norfolk in May, and in June I was ordered back to the West Coast and took command of VF-1 again for a year.

---

*David S. Ingalls was Assistant Secretary of the Navy (Aviation) from March 1929 to June 1932. Back in September 1918, he had become the Navy's first ace by scoring his fifth aerial victory against the Germans.
**Commander Harry E. Holt, USN(Ret.). Holt, who had enlisted in the Navy in the 1920s, was commissioned in 1942.

Bogan #1 - 42

Q: My information says that your squadron won the aircraft efficiency award for excellence in bombing and gunnery, and you were 50% higher than the number two group.

Admiral Bogan: That's right. That was VF-3, and we won that thing hands down. It was a great squadron as far as pilots were concerned.

Q: This is the one that had the enlisted people in it?

Admiral Bogan: No, no. VF-2 had enlisted pilots.

Q: This is the officer one that was on the Lexington that went back to the East Coast?

Admiral Bogan: We transferred to the Langley and went up the East Coast, and of the 18 men in that squadron at that time, seven of them made flag rank, which is a pretty high percentage.

Q: Isn't it? I should say so.

Admiral Bogan: So they were a little better than pilots.

Q: They were better than somewhat, I should say so. Who were they? Yourself, of course . . .

Bogan #1 - 43

Admiral Bogan: Myself, Bob Pirie, who was my chief of staff during the war, Ernie Litch, Soucek, Heath, Rodee.* That's all I can remember.

Q: That's wonderful. Well, it's wonderful to have known so well the people that you later had to work with.

Admiral Bogan: Yes, it is.

Q: Because I would think many times you interpreted things knowing the man as well as what the actual orders might be.

Admiral Bogan: Pirie was the superintendent of training at Miami. He's a very able man, one of the best.

Q: Is that the best group you ever worked with?

Admiral Bogan: The best small group I ever worked with, yes. No question about it.

Q: It's astonishing that out of 18, seven became admirals.

---
*Lieutenant (junior grade) Robert B. Pirie, USN, whose oral history is in the Naval Institute collection; Lieutenant Ernest W. Litch, USN; Lieutenant Apollo Soucek, USN; Lieutenant John P. Heath, USN; Lieutenant (junior grade) Walter F. Rodee, USN.

Bogan #1 - 44

Admiral Bogan: That's right.

Q: The VF-1 was . . ?

Admiral Bogan: It was attached to the Saratoga, and we spent from '31 until the spring of '32 in the Saratoga. An interesting part of that year is the fact that on a very early Sunday morning, taking off about 4:00 o'clock, off Honolulu, in very bad weather we made an attack, during a war game, on Oahu. That was February of '32.* In December '41, the Japanese copied that attack with results that are much better known.

Q: Who was the commanding officer of the Saratoga?

Admiral Bogan: It was Frank McCrary, but the admiral in charge of the fleet at that time, the carriers in the fleet, was Admiral Yarnell, who was a very superior naval officer in every way.**

Q: That war game was played more than once, wasn't it--which included the bombing of Oahu?

---

*For a more detailed account of this mock attack on Hawaii, see Admiral Arthur W. Radford, USN(Ret.), "Aircraft Battle Force," in Air Raid: Pearl Harbor! Recollections of a Day of Infamy (Annapolis: Naval Institute Press, 1981).
**Captain Frank R. McCrary, USN; Rear Admiral Harry E. Yarnell, USN, Commander Aircraft Battle Force.

Bogan #1 - 45

Admiral Bogan: At various times and under various circumstances, but this was the first time that a carrier had attacked Oahu.

Q: How far away had they taken off from? About the same distance as the Japanese?

Admiral Bogan: No, not as far as the Japs. We were about 100 miles away. The Japs were about 250 miles-300 miles away, to the north. We were northwest. A few days later, we were to go in and cover some bombers who were making a daylight attack on Oahu, and I had orders to cover for these men. A group of Army bombers and fighters came out to attack the fleet, and two of my pilots detached themselves from formation and fought these Army fighters all the way down to sea level, with me screaming on the radio for them to return. When I got back to the Saratoga after this thing, Admiral Yarnell said to me, "Bogan, Your communications were very good this morning. I think I could hear you without a radio."

Q: Why had they done that? Just for the hell of it?

Admiral Bogan: Enthusiasm. Sure.

Q: Everybody liked the idea, really, didn't they?

Admiral Bogan: Oh, sure. We had orders to stay there, and two of them piled off.

Q: Aviators have a special flair, I think, for living and excitement, which isn't true of other parts of the service.

Admiral Bogan: Those who have too much flair don't live to enjoy it.

Q: Is that true?

Admiral Bogan: You can only make one mistake, and in these planes today, the jet planes, every crash is fatal. When you think of the speed and the weight of these things. We could make mistakes and walk away from them. They can't. I was out on the Ticonderoga and Oriskany for two days several years ago, and watched them flying around the clock. And last January I went to Honolulu in the Enterprise with Admiral Cagle, who used to be my flag secretary, and I tell you she is an unbelievable ship, and the skill of that air group was just something I couldn't believe when when I was watching.* Let's say we paved the way, but I doubt that even as a young man I could have had the reaction time that these kids have to have to do the things they do 24 hours

---

*Rear Admiral Malcolm W. Cagle, USN, Commander Carrier Division One.

round the clock.

Q: Admiral Stroop said something that perhaps would interest you if you didn't know it--that similar tests have been made of pilots landing and their reactions, like they learned from the astronauts, and that the highest point of excitement is when these aviators land on a carrier, even more so than when they are actually doing the bombing.*

Admiral Bogan: Oh, I would think that. You've got, maybe now, I'd say, ten seconds where you've got to be absolutely right or you don't land. Of course, with the offset deck, if you don't land, you go around and do it again. If you were high coming in before the offset deck, you ran into the barriers.**

Q: Can you describe what it's like landing on a carrier?

Admiral Bogan: It's not an unusual sensation. You know you're right. You know you're going to catch the second or third wire. If you're wrong, but not too wrong, you're going to catch the

---
*Vice Admiral Paul D. Stroop, USN, whose oral history is in the Naval Institute collection.
**In the 1950s, U.S. aircraft carriers began to be equipped with angled flight decks for landing. Prior to that, on straight-deck carriers, a barrier was erected forward of the landing area to stop airplanes which missed the arresting wires during the course of landing aboard.

fifth or sixth. And the minute you land, you know you're in the arresting gear. The wires catch your tailhook, and you have an augmented deceleration, maybe, with these planes in 160 feet from 140 knots to zero, with our planes, maybe, 100 feet from 75 knots to zero. But it's not a disquieting or an uncomfortable situation.

Q: I'm sure if it were you couldn't repeat it. I mean, you couldn't stay and be an aviator, if it disturbed you.

Admiral Bogan: No. Now, I've known many people who've been afraid to fly, but have stayed in because they think that it's a sign of cowardice to get out. The bravest thing they could do, if they don't feel comfortable, is to ask for detachment from aviation duty, because everybody in the squadron knows that those people are uncomfortable in the air. They just feel sorry for them.

Q: Well, they're endangering others besides themselves.

Admiral Bogan: That's correct, yes.

Q: Did you ever know anybody who stayed in and shouldn't have?

Admiral Bogan: Yes, I've known several. One of the most honest was a friend of mine who was at Pensacola when I was an instructor, and he said, "I think I'll turn in my suit."

I said, "Why do you want to do it, Phipps?"

He said, "Because I feel so goddamned lonesome up there." An honest answer.

Q: Of course, and I would think one would. It would either be a terrible exhilaration or a--I can understand that lonesomeness. Did you find it exhilarating?

Admiral Bogan: Yes, I did. Let me put it this way--of course, the blackshoe people have always objected to aviators getting flight pay, and I'll say that 99% of the time you don't earn that flight pay.* But there comes a moment in everybody's career, sometimes several months, it may not last long for some of them, when you earn that flight pay several times over.

Q: Do they still resent it? I know that at the time you began aviation there was a real conflict between the two.

Admiral Bogan: Oh, yes. I don't know whether they resent it. The rules have been changed, and senior aviators who no longer fly combat planes don't get the same flight pay that the kids in

---
*Blackshoes are naval officers who specialize in surface ships--battleships, cruisers, and destroyers.

the squadron do, which is excellent. Having been retired as long as I have, I'm not familiar with the exact setup.

Q: Did you ever see any examples of reactions between the blackshoes and the aviators? I'm sure you saw it at the time.

Admiral Bogan: Well, when I first went into aviation, the blackshoes had an adjective to describe aviators, just as the southerner had to describe Yankees--goddamned Yankees--goddamned aviators.

Q: That just automatically went along.

Admiral Bogan: Yes, it did.

Q: And how long were you on the Saratoga?

Admiral Bogan: One year, at that time--from '31 to the spring of '32.

Q: And then where did you go from the Saratoga?

Admiral Bogan: I went to the Naval Air Station Anacostia as chief of Navy test pilots' section.

Q: What kind of planes were you testing?

Admiral Bogan: We were testing all the new planes that were being built for the Navy before they were approved and built in quantity for the fleet.

Q: Do you remember what kind they were?

Admiral Bogan: There was the first plane that Grumman built--the first fighter-scout plane that Grumman built for the Navy. There were several that Chance-Vought built for the Navy, scouting planes. There were fighter planes that Boeing built, and bombing planes that Douglas and Chance-Vought built.

Q: Did you have any near-misses with those?

Admiral Bogan: No.

Q: Did you like that duty?

Admiral Bogan: Very much.

Q: It was dangerous, wasn't it?

Admiral Bogan: I don't think so, not if you are sensibly

progressive about what you're trying to accomplish. I used to tell students at Pensacola that the best way for them to survive and succeed was never to overestimate their own ability nor the capabilities of the plane that they were flying. Put those two together within reasonable limits and you will get along.

Q: Were those the principles you followed?

Admiral Bogan: I tried to.

Q: You were the flight test officer there then?

Admiral Bogan: Yes.

Q: You were there, what, two years?

Admiral Bogan: Yes.

Q: Did you have to turn back any of the planes that they tried to sell the Navy?

Admiral Bogan: I'll tell you one little incident about that. There was one little experimental plane which was supposed to go aboard a submarine, have its wings folded and be put into a sort of auxiliary conning tower, and Grover Loening, who built it,

Bogan #1 - 53

brought the plane down and he also brought a six-weeks-old dachshund puppy. To make a long story short, we kept the dog and rejected the airplane.

Q: Did you fly that plane?

Admiral Bogan: Yes, surely we flew it, but we found it wasn't suitable for the work we wanted it to do.

Q: You never flew it from a submarine?

Admiral Bogan: No, no. From just testing it in the waters around Anacostia.

Q: Who did you say built that plane?

Admiral Bogan: Grover Loening.

Q: That wasn't this dachshund, I take it?

Admiral Bogan: No, no.

Q: We were just about to leave Anacostia.

Admiral Bogan: In the summer of '34, I went to the Lexington as assistant air officer, and after a year in that job moved up to air officer.

Q: This was the first time that you had not been attached with a squadron?

Admiral Bogan: Yes.

Q: How did you find that? Did you enjoy it? Did you like it? As compared to being with a squadron?

Admiral Bogan: Well, it's entirely different. It's the first step into what you might call an administrative job. I was 40 years old, and the captain did not think much of the man who was air officer, so he sort of had me run the show. It was the same as being air officer without the title, and the next year I became the air officer. So I spent two years in that department. It was very interesting. We had a pretty good record as a ship, as things go. Of the two carriers, the Lexington and the Saratoga, the Lexington was always much stricter. She was what we call a "taut ship," as you know she would be because Captain King was in command. The Saratoga was a little more on the lax side and perhaps a little more comfortable to live in, but, on the other hand, perhaps not as good a fighting ship as the Lexington was. I'm saying this as impersonally as I can, because

I've been in both of them.

Q: You say the Saratoga was not as good a fighting ship as the Lexington?

Admiral Bogan: She was not as well administered, and Navy discipline was not as strict in the Saratoga as it was in the Lexington.

Q: Was Captain King then the CO of the Lexington when you were air officer?

Admiral Bogan: No. Captain Cook was commanding officer of the Lexington, except for the last three months, when Captain Fitch relieved him.*

Q: You spoke of Captain King as related to the Lexington.

Admiral Bogan: He had been the commanding officer from '30 until '32.

Q: I see, and the procedures he set up continued under other commanding officers. I'd like to have you tell me about being

---

*Captain Arthur B. Cook, USN, was relieved as commanding officer in 1936 by Captain Aubrey W. Fitch, USN.

air officer and what you did. What were your duties?

Admiral Bogan: The air officer of a ship is responsible for all the activities in the air department: the servicing of the planes, the launching, the landing, the respotting on deck, inspections when they come back to see if they're ready for the next flight, and to arrange the schedules on training days of what the air plan shall do. The latter, of course, approved by the captain.

Q: And did you do that yourself?

Admiral Bogan: Yes.

Q: How many squadrons were on the Lexington then?

Admiral Bogan: There were four. There were two fighter squadrons, a bombing squadron, and a torpedo squadron.

Q: And you enjoyed that duty, too?

Admiral Bogan: Yes, I enjoyed it very much. It was interesting work.

Q: Did you feel that it was administratively or professionally a step up in your career?

Admiral Bogan: Yes, I thought it was a step along, because in spite of the fact that--we were all getting along toward the age where we would command a carrier, and the Morrow Board in 1925 had specified that carriers could be commanded only by naval aviators.*

Q: Don't you think that was a good idea?

Admiral Bogan: Yes, I do. I hesitate to think what it would be if they weren't. For instance, in the Fleet Air Arm of the British Navy, they have blackshoes commanding carriers. I know of one British carrier where the captain had the barriers taken down--which stopped the planes--because he said they were a mental hazard to the pilot.

Q: That's hard to believe.

Admiral Bogan: It may be hard to believe, but it's a fact.

---

*In 1925, an air policy board was chaired by Dwight Morrow, later the father-in-law of flier Charles Lindbergh. In 1926 legislation resulting from the Morrow Report produced several changes, including the requirement that aircraft carriers, seaplane tenders, and naval air stations be commanded by naval aviators.

Q: Did you do any operations of any particular interest that you recall while you were on the Lexington?

Admiral Bogan: No, they were just the routine fiscal year training operations. Qualification of new pilots from time to time, but nothing out of the ordinary.

Q: Are there any anecdotes that you particularly recall? You've been now on the Saratoga, the Lexington, and the Langley, all the three early carriers. That's quite a record in itself, isn't it?

Admiral Bogan: No. It's no record. It just happened to have occurred.

Q: And then you went from the Lexington to Pensacola?

Admiral Bogan: Superintendent of training at Pensacola for a year, and executive officer for a year.

Q: Did you introduce any new ideas into this training?

Admiral Bogan: No, but the training had greatly expanded, because the naval aviation cadet program had started the year before I reported as superintendent. We had all these young college boys who were qualified, and they were a magnificent lot.

They'd been screened, maybe, down to 10% of the original applicants before they were enrolled, and they were a magnificent lot of people.

Q: How long was their training?

Admiral Bogan: Same as the regular course, plus a lot of naval indoctrination added into it. They had schools and things like that.

Q: Was there any feeling this early of the imminence of war?

Admiral Bogan: No, I wouldn't say so. I had it in '38, before the war actually started, but we were just going along, fat, dumb, and happy.

Q: I wondered if the thought of war was why they started the cadet program.

Admiral Bogan: No, because the output of the Naval Academy would not supply the needs--the naval aviators that we needed and the line duty naval officers to man the fleet. The increase had been coming for a long time, and finally this was enacted. At first, under the regulation, these young men were restricted to naval aviation duties only. They went aboard ship, and when they weren't flying they weren't doing anything. They had no responsible jobs, and finally when a few enterprising captains got them up as junior officers of the deck, they found out to their surprise that because of the acuteness of these kids, they made better officers of the deck than regular officers who were normally assigned to it. And the regulations were loosened, so they became a part of the ship's organization. In 1940, I was a member of the selection board which was convened to inspect these young men for commissions in the regular Navy; at that time they were Naval Reservists. We took about 98% of them into the regular Navy, and they just went on from there.

Q: Properly so, it would seem.

Admiral Bogan: Very properly so, but too late, as usual.

Q: Why do you say "too late"?

Admiral Bogan: Because they should have recognized the fact that these people were good material from the beginning and not restrict them to aviation duties only for so long. And a great many of them got out after their first obligated tour was up, because they had been.

Q: That's what I was wondering. The obvious thing is that we lost many because we didn't handle them properly.

Admiral Bogan: Yes.

Q: Were any of the senior officers at Pensacola at the time that you were there as exec?

Admiral Bogan: As students?

Q: I was thinking of the time when Admiral King and Admiral Halsey . . .

Admiral Bogan: One was there. Captain McCain.* He had interrupted his training to make the cruise with us in the <u>Lexington</u> the year before, and his instructor came to me and said, "Commander, I'm afraid of Captain McCain--his progress here." I had had occasion to knock this instructor out at Pearl Harbor several years before when he pulled something I didn't like, and I mean knock him out with my fist, not . . .

Q: Oh, oh, I wondered what you meant.

Admiral Bogan: So he came round and told me this, and I said,

---

*Captain John S. McCain, USN, later Commander Task Force 38 in World War II.

"All right. Will you tell that to the commandant tomorrow morning?:

"Yes."

"All right. 10:00 o'clock." So I brought him in to Admiral Blakely who was the commandant, and I said, "Admiral, Allen would like to comment on Captain McCain's progress."*

He said, "Go ahead."

"Oh," he said, "he's doing just fine, sir." I think this fellow was trying to get back at me for something that had happened several years before.

So the commandant said, "What are you wasting my time for here, Bogan?" In the next two weeks before he graduated, McCain cracked up five airplanes.

Q: What did you do? What was your reaction?

Admiral Bogan: What could I do? I was the superintendent of training. I couldn't recommend that he . . .

Admiral Bogan: Were there any other senior officers at Pensacola during that period?

Admiral Bogan: At that time, no.

---
*Rear Admiral Charles A. Blakely, USN, commandant of the naval air station at Pensacola, Florida.

Q: Then that was more responsibility, too, as exec of that very large station, wasn't it?

Admiral Bogan: Yes. Admiral Halsey was the commandant while I was exec. He relieved Blakely, and I spent the last year there as his exec.

Q: What was your relationship with him?

Admiral Bogan: Very friendly and very cooperative. He was a very fine man. Not a mastermind, by any means, but a very sound, fine person.

Q: Was he a good commandant?

Admiral Bogan: Yes, I think so.

Q: He was what, did you say, when he learned to fly?

Admiral Bogan: Fifty-one, and he went from there to command the Saratoga.

Q: Then you went back to sea?

Admiral Bogan: I went back as navigator of the Yorktown in '38, and Admiral Halsey became a division commander of that carrier division which consisted of the Yorktown and Enterprise. After a year as navigator, I moved up to executive officer under Captain Gunther in June of 1940.*

Q: By this time there was the feeling of war in the air, wasn't there?

Admiral Bogan: We participated in one long fleet engagement in the Caribbean, and came to Norfolk to resupply, and we were supposed to go to New York. But because of some incident or act which I have forgotten, which the Japanese had committed in the Pacific, we were ordered immediately to the Pacific. We went through the canal and up to San Diego and San Francisco.

Q: And war, of course, was going on in Europe by this time.

Admiral Bogan: No, this was before the war. This was in the spring of '39, but the war clouds were there and had been there ever since Munich.**

---
*Captain Ernest L. Gunther, USN.
**In September 1938, at Munich, Bavaria, Britain, and France agreed to Adolf Hitler's demand for the cession of the Sudentenland from Czechoslovakia to Germany in return for a "guarantee" of peace. In later years, the Munich conference came to symbolize appeasement of a dictator.

Q: Was there a feeling in the fleet--did you ever have a feeling of offensive urgency at this time, or were people still going along in the usual routine?

Admiral Bogan: They had a sense of concern, let's say.

Q: This time as exec, were you a captain then?

Admiral Bogan: No. I was a commander.

Q: When did you make captain?

Admiral Bogan: The day after Pearl Harbor.

Q: Did you ever have any trouble with your promotion?

Admiral Bogan: Never.

Q: Can you tell me any anecdotes or any of the activities of the Yorktown?

Admiral Bogan: I can tell you one that's a little amusing. My first skipper in the Yorktown was a man named McWhorter, who was a very gregarious, friendly man.* He'd been in submarines and

---
*Captain Ernest D. McWhorter, USN.

was one of the late arrivals in aviation. As long as we were in port, he was very pleasant, but he was so nervous at sea that being navigator and on the bridge with him 20 hours a day was a long watch. One day in the Caribbean, we were landing planes, and we had about four more to put on the deck. There was a very light wind, and we were making perhaps 28 knots. Up ahead of us was one of these little tropical showers with a rainbow through it, nothing serious. And Mac began to worry about what to do, so I said, "Captain, there will be a few drops of rain on the planes. It won't bother the pilots at all. Just go ahead with the landing."

He got more and more concerned and finally said, "I think I'll go down and ask the admiral." So he went down to the flag bridge where Admiral Halsey was, and I thought Halsey would throw him off the ship. So I leaned over the railing of the ladder to see what would happen, and all he said was, "Well, Mac, I don't care. If you're not in a hurry, why don't you go around. It'll only take a few minutes." The decision had been made for him, and Mac's face lighted up like a Christmas tree, and he got to the first step of the ladder and said, "Admiral, shall I use right or left rudder?"

Q: Oh, not really? How long did he last as a skipper?

Admiral Bogan: Halsey's aide told me that afternoon Halsey was so mad, he said, "I'll see that he never gets promoted." But he was promoted, or at least he was selected, but when he took his physical they found out he had a double hernia and said he'd have to be operated. He was so afraid to be operated on that he held off for eight months, and they told him if he didn't have the operation, they'd take him off the list the next week. So he had the operation, which wasn't serious, and then he had one duty as admiral during the war. He was in the Ranger in the African landing attacks. I wasn't there, but a lot of things must have been wrong, because he came ashore right after that and never went to sea again.

Q: That poor devil was scared out of his life. What a miserable life he must have led! How could he be a skipper of an aircraft carrier? It's hard to believe, isn't it?

Admiral Bogan: That was when they used to assign them by so-called qualification. Here he had Pensacola qualification, so they assigned him to it.

Q: You were aware, of course, all the time of his inadequacy?

Admiral Bogan: I spent 20 hours a day on the bridge with him when we were under way.

Q: To be sure that nothing happened to the ship?

Admiral Bogan: You learn a lot in 20 hours.

Q: Of course, you do.

Admiral Bogan: And when you do it time after time, it gets pretty long.

Q: Twenty hours a day. Now tell me about that. You mean you stood your own watch plus his?

Admiral Bogan: I wasn't standing watches.

Q: No, I know that.

Admiral Bogan: Under regular conditions, I'd get up at 4:00 o'clock in the morning for morning star sights. And we'd be in formation all day, and the navigator has to be on the bridge for formation. Then take the sights in the evening, write out the night orders for his signature, and then go up until the duty commander came on--that was 10:00 or 12:00 o'clock--and back again at 4:00 o'clock the next morning.

Q: So it really was a 20-hour day.

Admiral Bogan: Sure.

Q: How long did you keep that up?

Admiral Bogan: As long as necessary.

Q: Weren't you exhausted?

Admiral Bogan: No.

Q: It's a pretty rough schedule.

Admiral Bogan: It was.

Q: Could you take no time off during the day?

Admiral Bogan: I might go back, if things were quiet and we were alone, into my own little cabin, which was just off the bridge. And I'd read and sometimes turn in for an hour or so, but as a rule it was a straight 4:00 to 12:00.

Q: Have you any other stories of that period?

Admiral Bogan: No.

Bogan #1 - 70

Q: You spoke of being in the Caribbean during part of that time?

Admiral Bogan: From January until May of '39 we were in the Caribbean, and the fleet exercise probably took three weeks of that time.

Q: Was that during the time when you said you went back because of some incident that the Japanese . . .

Admiral Bogan: After these fleet exercises were over, the fleet came up to the East Coast and we refueled and re-stored and re-provisioned in Norfolk. We were due to go to New York, but there was something that happened in the Pacific. The fleet was suddenly ordered immediately from Norfolk to the West Coast again.

Q: But did you go on out to Pearl?

Admiral Bogan: No.

Q: Stayed on the West Coast? We're covering your career awfully fast. I hope you're not leaving out anything.

Admiral Bogan: No, nothing worthwhile.

Bogan #1 - 71

Q: Yes, it is. It's always worthwhile. Then we're going to continue on with your new duties as executive officer of the Yorktown.

Admiral Bogan: In June, I became executive officer, and Captain Gunther became commanding officer. We had a rather routine year on the West Coast, terminated by a fleet exercise in Honolulu, following which we went to Bremerton Navy Yard for quick dry-docking, and I was detached and ordered to Washington for temporary duty.* After six weeks in Washington, I was ordered to take command of the naval air station in Miami, for which ground had just been broken, and for the next two years I commanded that station.

Q: Tell me about that.

Admiral Bogan: It was assuming the responsibility of training carrier pilots after their basic training at Pensacola, while the station at Corpus Christi was being built.

Q: Did you take over all of the carrier training from Pensacola, then?

---
*Known officially as the Puget Sound Navy Yard, Bremerton, Washington.

Admiral Bogan: Yes, all of the carrier training from Pensacola, both the Navy and Marines, and the course at Miami required about two months. It was a very interesting job, and I think the taxpayer got his dollar back, because no group of people that I've ever known worked harder in the daytime or played harder at night than at Miami.

Q: How large a station was it? Both in area and the numbers of personnel?

Admiral Bogan: I would say the area was, perhaps, 600 acres. We had one field to land and another to take off from, depending on the direction of the wind, and with the maintenance, the hangars, and the administration in the center of the area. There were quarters for only six senior officers on the station. The rest of them lived in various places in Miami. And we also trained British pilots for the Fleet Air Arm. To show you what difficult straits they were--most of our students had driven an automobile and had some mechanical ability, and at the time I left to take command of the Saratoga in October of '42, we had graduated 2,900 American pilots, and we'd had ten fatalities. We'd graduated 200 British students and had ten fatalities. In other words, the rate was greater than ten to one. As an example of the straits to which the British were reduced, I was in the training superintendent's office one day when a British pilot was being considered for extra time, and Pirie, the superintendent of training, said, "What was your experience? What did you do in England before you entered this program?"*

He said, "I was a draper's assistant, sir," which means in English--in Americanese--that he had worked in a cleaning store. It was just too bad. They tried hard, and once they became proficient, they were great, but they had very little basis to start on.

Q: I've read things about that, that basically the American boy, man, person, is a tinkerer from the time he's a child and probably adjusts to mechanical things easier.

Admiral Bogan: They did, and, of course, they'd lost so many. After World War I, the caliber of the average British citizen was very much like that of France, deteriorated, and the British Empire deteriorated even faster.

Q: They just lost so many people.

Admiral Bogan: That's it. They lost the cream of their youth.

Q: Sure. A tragedy, of course, all along. Did any of the

---
*Lieutenant Commander Robert B. Pirie, USN. Pirie's oral history is in the Naval Institute collection.

people from the naval air station in Miami do any patrols or any antisubmarine work at all, or was it all training?

Admiral Bogan: We did occasional patrols when we were called upon during the worst part of the submarine menace in the Gulf Stream. In the summer, of course, there were being set up at Jacksonville and at Key West definite antisubmarine patrol commands at that time. We had nothing but training planes and no skill in combat, and the only way we could do anything was visual sighting and report. But all through the summer of 1942, the Gulf Stream off Miami was a sea of fire at night from flaming tankers which the submarines were sinking. It's true. You'd see three or four at a time, ten miles offshore burning.

Q: To whom would the patrols from your station report?

Admiral Bogan: The submarine command at Key West would request, not order, that we conduct such patrols as were possible, and we would do so. But I wouldn't say that they were ever of any value, because we didn't have the material, we didn't have the trained pilots to do that sort of thing.

Q: Nor was the device for sighting developed at that point, was it? You were talking about carriers.

Admiral Bogan: No. Of course, the antisubmarine patrol used sonar buoys which would come in the water and float and reflect the noise from a submarine, but we had nothing of that sort.

Q: You had none of the equipment.

Admiral Bogan: Our patrols were a gesture and useless, such as they were. I had two or three conferences with the Duke of Windsor, who was then governor of the Bahamas, and one time I suggested, "Would you like us to send some planes over there to help you offshore?"*

And I then realized how impotent the once-King of England was when he said, "Yes, I think that might be a good idea, but first I would have to get the cooperation of my Parliament," which, of course, was Negro.

Q: Was this the Duke of Windsor?

Admiral Bogan: Yes, the same one.

Q: So you didn't ever furnish him with any patrols?

Admiral Bogan: No, we didn't, because he didn't ask for them.

---

*The Duke of Windsor was the former King Edward VIII, living in exile following his 1936 abdication.

Q: Well, you actually then established this station and you stayed there two years after it was established?

Admiral Bogan: That's right. We broke ground on the 15th of August, and with a very unfinished station but with skeleton facilities we began our first training on the fourth of October, which I think is a very short period to start an air station.

Q: How many instructors did you have?

Admiral Bogan: We increased them gradually as the need occurred, and I've forgotten now, but we were able to handle all of our students with adequate instruction.

Q: I wanted to ask you, though, before we left that, where you were and how you heard about Pearl Harbor.

Admiral Bogan: I was having lunch at a hotel on the beach--Miami Beach--about 1:00 o'clock, December seventh, and one of the guests left early to go out and get his hat and go home. And he came running back and said, "The Japs have attacked Pearl Harbor." That was my first intimation.

Q: What was your reaction to that? How did you feel?

Admiral Bogan: I was very stupid. I said, "Well, that war will probably last nine months."

Q: What made you say that?

Admiral Bogan: Because I didn't know how good the Japs were, and I thought we were better than we were.

Q: What was your emotional reaction? Excitement? Upset?

Admiral Bogan: No, I don't think there was any emotional reaction. The time had come to do what I'd been trained to do for a good many years, and I hoped I'd be able to do it.

Q: Did your station change in its operations?

Admiral Bogan: Not ostensibly. Although it was entirely unnecessary in my point of view, I knew that if something happened I had the responsibility, so we'd scatter the planes around at night on the field, doubled the security watches, and conformed to the blackout, which was immediately put on in Miami, properly in the city of Miami. In other words, we darkened up and we tightened things considerably, but there was very little we could do, except for saboteurs, and we took steps that we thought would prevent any such sabotage and there was none.

Q: Was there any increase in the submarine activity off the coast?

Admiral Bogan: Not at that time. That became evident in the late spring. The summer of '42, as I've told you before, was-- they were in the Gulf Stream and in the channel between Key West and Havana and even into the Gulf of Mexico. And the carnage of ships was terrific.

Q: That was before you left?

Admiral Bogan: That was before I left, yes. I left on the first of October.

Q: And then you went to the Saratoga?

Admiral Bogan: Yes.

Q: Were those orders requested by you?

Admiral Bogan: No, but I'd been hoping for them for a long time, and they came in the latter part of September. I left on the first of October for Pearl Harbor. The Saratoga at that time was in dry dock, having been torpedoed about a month before off Guadalcanal, that area, and I relieved Duke Ramsey, who had been commanding officer and who was later commanding officer of the task group of which the Saratoga was a unit.* After a short training period . . .

Q: Where was the Saratoga when you took over?

Admiral Bogan: In Pearl Harbor dry dock. After a short training period of about four days, we left Pearl Harbor for the South Pacific, with a fueling stop at Nandi in the Fiji Islands, and then proceeded to Noumea in New Caledonia, where I reported to Admiral Halsey, who was commander in the South Pacific at that time. The next seven months were spent in patrols off, south of, and in the vicinity of Guadalcanal, supporting the operations there. On two occasions, we sent the air group in to be based for a day or two at Guadalcanal. We saw very little enemy opposition, and our total bag of Japanese planes during the seven months that I had the Saratoga was seven Bettys, which we managed to intercept with our combat air patrols and shoot down.**

Q: Where were you then?

---
*Captain DeWitt C. Ramsey, USN, commanding officer of the Saratoga (CV-3) from May 1942 until relieved in October of that same year by Captain Bogan.
**Betty was the Allied code name for the Japanese Navy Mitsubishi G4M land-based medium bomber.

Admiral Bogan: In the South Pacific, in the Coral Sea.

Q: You weren't in the Battle of the Coral Sea?

Admiral Bogan: No, but in that area.

Q: What operations were going on then?

Admiral Bogan: Most of the operations had to do with the resupply and reinforcement of Guadalcanal proper, from which raids were then being conducted up the Slot on Munda and sometimes as far as Bougainville on the other end. Except when my air group was ashore, we had nothing to do with that. We were sort of preventive medicine south of Guadalcanal to prevent any Japanese attack from an unexpected direction.

Q: Were you in any of the battles going up the Solomons?

Admiral Bogan: No, we were not, because, as I say, the last battle in the Solomons took place on the 14th of November, when two of the cruisers of this task group of which the Saratoga was a unit were detached at Nandi and ordered to join a group off the Solomons, and they were very badly mauled by a Japanese force on the night of November 14th. We came down with a couple of destroyers and reported to Admiral Halsey at Noumea.

Bogan #1 - 81

Q: Where were you when the Japanese planes tried to attack you?

Admiral Bogan: Well, they were just scattered patrols that--and with the Japanese tendency to do things at a set time, they ran a set patrol from Kavieng every day on a certain route, and having intercepted them on that route on two days, they would probably be there tomorrow, so we did the same thing, and on three successive days we shot down the entire patrol. Then they stopped it.

Q: Isn't that interesting? Now, it was on the Saratoga that you were injured, wasn't it?

Admiral Bogan: It was my own fault. In March of '43, I had been ordered up to take command of the naval air force--it was a combined air force--at Guadalcanal. While we were anchored or moored in Noumea one night, the duty commander came in and said, "We expect heavy weather." Occasionally the mooring chains would foul or get twisted, so after dinner I went up to the bow with a flashlight in my hand--it was raining heavily, the ship was darkened--to see if the chains were clear and we could let go in a hurry if it were necessary to get out. While I was up there, I dropped my flashlight, saw the chains were clear, came back. And as I was about to step on a ladder to go down one deck to my cabin, I must have tripped on the forward arresting gear slot, because the next thing I knew was four days later I was on the Solace, a hospital ship, en route to Auckland. I had tripped and fallen off the flight deck and hit the back of my head on a 40-millimeter gun director 10 feet below. I had a slight linear fracture and a very heavy concussion.

Q: How long were you out of commission?

Admiral Bogan: As soon as the Solace got under way, before it began to turn, I became completely conscious.

Q: Tell me what happened while you were on the hospital ship.

Admiral Bogan: Well, apparently I had periods of lucidity, because one day while some officer of the Saratoga was over to see me, I got up from my bunk to get a pack of cigarettes and a nurse came in, a very attractive girl, and she said, "You get right back into bed, Captain."

And I'm reported to have said, "After you, dear."

When Admiral Halsey heard that, he said, "I knew Jerry was all right."

Q: And you said the story preceded you . . .

Admiral Bogan: The story got back to the West Coast and also to my wife, and I had a little explaining to do, which, of course, has never been resolved.

Q: I think that's a very humorous story. How long were you on the hospital ship?

Admiral Bogan: I was in the hospital in Auckland for four weeks, and when I reported there, this Reserve Navy doctor named Blood from Los Angeles, said, "You're going to have to stay in bed for ten days."*

I said, "All right. I shall." And I did. The original diagnosis was correct. It said "compound fracture of the skull and intracranial injury," which means brain damage. The hospital commanding officer was a good friend of mine, and he showed me these pictures, and it was just a simple linear crack with no depression. So at the end of ten days, this doctor didn't come around, and at the end of 12 days, this doctor didn't come around, so I stopped using a bed pan and went across the corridor to the showers and to the head, and he appeared at the end of 15 days and said, "You've been up."

So I said, "Yes. You told me to stay in bed for ten days."

He said, "I told you ten, but I meant 20."

So I said, "Why didn't you tell me?"

---
*Lieutenant Commander Russell H. Blood, MC, USNR.

An amusing incident occurred out of that. One night when I had made myself some coffee and was sitting there--the rest of this ward was filled with convalescent or ambulatory Marines who had been up at Guadalcanal and had malaria and things like that, and the partitions between the bunks were about 6 feet high. This nurse came by and said, "May I share a coffee with you?"

I said, "Certainly. Get yourself a cup." So we sat there, and she sat for about 40 minutes, and I thought, "It's not my invalid attractions that are keeping you here; there's some ulterior motive." Anyway, she got up and left. The next night the same thing happened, and she'd been there about ten minutes, when a Marine about three bunks down came back in. She put her coffee cup down, and a very terrific fight started. Apparently she made the mistake of asking the $64 question, when she said, "What have these goddamned New Zealand girls got that I haven't got?"

He said, "Nothing, darling, but they use theirs."

So after four weeks in the hospital, I came back on the _Matsonia_, which was the old _Malolo_, to San Diego, and reported to the hospital.* I had a complete physical examination, and a complete flight examination, and passed with flying colors, and a board of medical survey, which I passed with flying colors.

---

*The Matson Navigation Company's 17,226-gross ton, 554-foot liner _Matsonia_ had been the _Malolo_ prior to being renamed in 1937.

Then, because the Navy had nominated General Hale to be the Air Corps commander of the antisubmarine warfare which was part of the Tenth Fleet in Washington, and the Navy wanted somebody of similar rank across from him--I had been promoted from captain to rear admiral in January, but had not been sworn in--so I was ordered to Washington as Commander Naval Air Tenth Fleet, on Admiral King's staff. I knew nothing about this at the time, but this original diagnosis of compound fracture and intracranial injury had me under suspicion for six months. Even my best friends in the Medical Corps wouldn't tell me, but I was under suspicion. Later medical knowledge proved that people with similar injuries, if they could be got on their feet and lead a normal life sooner, were much more probable recoveries. This intracranial injury would indicate a blood clot, you see, which might cause paralysis. Under Navy pressure, the Army had withdrawn Hale's name, so there was no necessity for me to be there, and Admiral King said, "What do you think you should do in this job?"

And I said, "Admiral, without seeing the whole picture, I don't think I could do anything, and I think I'll go up to Argentia in Newfoundland, then all the way down to South America and see the picture firsthand."

And he said, "If you hadn't said that, I was going to tell you to do it." So I did. I spent three weeks on this trip.

Q: How did you travel?

Admiral Bogan: By naval air transport planes. I actually piloted the plane, a DC-3, 150 hours that month. Ended up in Panama, then came back to Miami. And because the report I wrote for Admiral King agreed with some of the things that he'd decided for himself, I was in his good graces temporarily, and he said, "I'll get you back to sea by the first of October," which was the six months, you see.

Q: Oh, yes.

Admiral Bogan: Then somebody suggested I be sent to the Azores in command of this new air station they were building.

Q: But wasn't the Tenth Fleet a new organization?

Admiral Bogan: The Tenth Fleet was really an administrative organization, run from Admiral King's headquarters right there in Washington, and it consisted of the antisubmarine weapons, mostly aircraft, the Eastern Sea Frontier, the Caribbean Sea Frontier, and the South Atlantic Sea Frontier. The general direction was under Admiral King's office, and he had quite a staff there of scientists and all the rest of them, and we had broken the code, and the previous May had been the backbreaking month for submarines, I think. There were 48 submarines sunk in March or May, and the rate of destruction was continuing.

So I went to him when this business about going to the Azores came up and I said, "You told me you'd send me to sea on the first of October."

"I will," he said, "when I'm goddamn good and ready."

Q: But before that, now what did you accomplish with the Tenth Fleet?

Admiral Bogan: I could advise Admiral King whether antisubmarine operations were effective, and where they were ineffective, and where I thought changes should be made. And they were worst in Admiral Andrews's district, who had their headquarters in New York.* He had a group of Wall Street people on his staff, non-aviators, and one time when I talked to his chief of staff, I said, "You've got this fellow Morris. He's ordering planes around, and he doesn't know anything about aviation."

He said, "He's going to get his wings and a private license next month."

I said, "We're talking about naval aviation, offensive antisubmarine warfare, and he's no good." I think that I earned my pay while I was there, and then in October a friend and

---
*Vice Admiral Adolphus Andrews, USN, Commandant Third Naval District and Commander Eastern Sea Frontier.

contemporary of King's, who had been relieved of a task group over in Scotland, two battleships and one carrier, said he wanted to go to the Pacific if he could pass the physical examination. And he could pass the physical examination, so King sent him to the job in the Pacific that he'd promised me, and he lasted a month. I was in Norfolk for two months, and finally in January . . .

Q: Why did he do that?

Admiral Bogan: Because this man was a friend of his, a contemporary of his, and he felt a little loyalty to him.

Q: But you say he had promised it to you?

Admiral Bogan: Well, he told me I could go to sea. He didn't promise me that particular job. So on the 21st of December, this message came down from Washington, the Bureau of Medicine and Surgery, and it said, "Send Bogan to the Norfolk Hospital [Portsmouth Hospital] for a complete physical examination, including neurological examination, and telephone report to Washington." So I went over, and there was a little Jew over there from Bellevue Hospital and a very good guy. I had passed five boards of medical survey by that time, and if my reactions weren't involuntary, I knew what they were supposed to be, so I could do them. He went all over my case, and he said, "Admiral, your original diagnosis in your case was wrong."

I said, I know that, but you're the only doctor besides my father that ever admitted that another doctor made a mistake." So they gave me a clean bill of health, but I still couldn't find out anything, so the next morning I flew up to Washington, and I found out that Putty Read, who had command of the NC-4 trip across the Atlantic, had enraged Mrs. Roosevelt by suggesting that no more blacks be sent to the training command at the Navy pier in Chicago, because there were 10,000 of them there and they were just raising hell criminally in Chicago.* Mrs. Roosevelt got hold of the Navy Department, the Secretary of the Navy, and said, "Read can't be in Chicago any longer." Maybe she got hold of the Secretary, Frank Knox. So because I had a very ineffectual job down at Norfolk and they were looking for a quiet place to send Putty, they sent him there, and I found that out through the grapevine in Washington. And I went down to Admiral King's office and I was going to tell him the truth about this thing. Of course, I knew who was going to relieve me, where I was going and all the rest of it. He said, "Hello, Jerry, what are you doing here?"

---

*Rear Admiral Albert C. Read, USN, chief of air technical training in Chicago from 1942 to 1944. In May 1919, then-Lieutenant Commander Read, naval aviator #24, made the first transatlantic crossing in the flying boat NC-4.

I thought, "Christ, if you're going to give me the runaround, I'll give it to you." And I said, "Nothing, Admiral, I just came in to wish you a merry Christmas," and that was it.

He said, "I'll tell you something now. You're on your way as soon as I can find a relief for you." I knew that he had the relief. I knew who it was going to be, and I knew when he was going to be there, see, but if you're going to have to dance around conversationally, I thought I'd dance, too.

Q: Sure. I would feel the same way, I think. Why was he being so cozy?

Admiral Bogan: I don't know. He knew but I didn't.

Q: You told me that at one time, later, you said to him that he did not think of you in a proper regard. Was this the incident you were talking about?

Admiral Bogan: Oh, no, no. I said that on the Lexington when I had this VF-3 squadron. All through the thing he just bawled me out all the time.

Q: Oh, I didn't know that.

Admiral Bogan: I told you this earlier in the tape. And I was no good and all the rest. Then when I saw my written record, that he had written out for me for that period, in the Bureau of Personnel I was superman, one of the best officers in the Navy. That's what he said on paper, but to me he said, "You're a no-good SOB," or words to that effect.

Q: Tell me again what he said about, if a fellow does a good job, you don't tell him so. What did he say about that?

Admiral Bogan: He said, "We've both gotten along, haven't we, in our separate ways? I'm too old to change mine." He was a very fine man.

Q: You told me, I think, off the tape that he said that people needed to be brought up short every six months or so.

Admiral Bogan: Well, to go into details on that action--we started out on a fleet exercise, the destroyer commanded by a classmate of mine, and had been at sea for two days as a sort of picket ship outside it. Some new instructions for destroyers fueled alongside had been issued which he had not received, being out there. So when he did come alongside, I went up to the bow and tied this sheet of paper to a heaving line and threw it over to him. He did it the old way, and King said, "Go off and do it again," so he read the thing, and came back and did it again. I was having lunch in the cabin with him that day, and I said, "You shouldn't have bawled him out for that. He didn't have those instructions. He knew nothing about them until I gave them to him."

He said, "I don't give a goddamn how good they are, unless they get a kick in the ass every six weeks, they slack off."

Q: This was the incident when he said that?

Admiral Bogan: Yes, that's when he said that.

Q: And then it was later, in 1947, when you saw him in the hallway that you reminded him of that incident.

Admiral Bogan: That's when he asked me to come into his office. That's the last time I ever saw him, before he had the stroke.

Q: Then you went into his office and he played cozy, so you figured you'd play the same game. Then how soon did you get orders after that?

Admiral Bogan: Two days.

Q: And where did they take you?

Bogan #1 - 93

Admiral Bogan: They took me to Commander Carrier Division 25, which was the division of the CVEs or jeep carriers, which were new ships just being organized.

Q: You were an admiral by now?

Admiral Bogan: I'd been an admiral all the time in the Tenth Fleet.

Q: Oh, yes.

Admiral Bogan: So we did a little antisubmarine patrol and . . .

Q: Where were you?

Admiral Bogan: At Pearl most of the time and some rehearsals for Saipan, and then . . .

Q: How many ships were in the group?

Admiral Bogan: Four in that division. I later had two more added to the group.

Q: What were the names of the ships?

Admiral Bogan: In that division, there was the Fanshaw Bay, the Kalinin Bay, the Midway, later renamed St. Lo and sunk just off Leyte, and the White Plains. Four days off Saipan, the Fanshaw Bay was bombed, and I sent her back for repairs and shifted to the White Plains, and spent the rest of the Saipan operation in the White Plains. At the end of the Saipan operation, we went back to Eniwetok, and I was ordered to the big carriers, Task Force 38, or 58, depending on whether Halsey or Spruance was in command, and I went aboard the Essex as my flagship.*

Q: Tell me what happened off Saipan. Were your CVEs--you were commander of Carrier Division 25, and that was the CVEs, and you said much of the time you operated out of Pearl, and then you . . .

Admiral Bogan: No. Before this. Until the 15th of May when we started out for Saipan, we operated out of Pearl in preparing, shaking down these new ships. Then on the way to Saipan, we stopped at Eniwetok and refueled, and arrived off Saipan on the morning of 15 June, and the whole time in the period of that three and a half week operation, these ships furnished air

---

*Task Force 38 was part of the Third Fleet, commanded by Admiral William F. Halsey, Jr., USN; Task Force 58 was part of the Fifth Fleet, commanded by Admiral Raymond A. Spruance, USN.

support for the land operations at Saipan. In other words, we had planes in the air all the time on call from the air control ship at Saipan, telling us to bomb certain targets. We also ran antisubmarine patrols round the entire force, and it was a compliment to me when General Shepherd told a friend of mine not long ago that in all the war they never got better coordinated air support than they got at Saipan on call from the ships.*

Q: And that was 15 June that . . ?

Admiral Bogan: From 15 June until the 12th of July, I think.

Q: And was that not called Operation Forager?

Admiral Bogan: That's right.

Q: And it was Admiral Spruance . . .

Admiral Bogan: Spruance was in command of the Fifth Fleet.

Q: Can you go on with more about the CVEs, about the Saipan operation?

---

*General Lemuel C. Shepherd, Jr., USMC(Ret.), who was Commandant of the Marine Corps, 1952-1955.

Admiral Bogan: Well, I can say this--that two of those four ships were very good. The Midway was commanded by a little fellow named Francis McKenna, who died about six weeks ago of cancer.* The Kalinin Bay was commanded by Cat Brown, who not long ago suffered a stroke.** I think he's pretty well recovered. The White Plains, to which I transferred, was a dud of a ship, and the original one, the Fanshaw Bay, was the worst ship I've ever seen in any Navy.

Q: What do you mean by that?

Admiral Bogan: She didn't do anything right. Nothing was right.

Q: How come?

Admiral Bogan: Because her skipper and the other people, with the exception of the air officer, I think the entire complement was incompetent.

Q: That's a good reason.

Admiral Bogan: I think it is. One later afternoon, the Japs had a big fleet of aircraft up from Guam to attack us, and that was

---
*Captain Francis J. McKenna, USN.
**Captain Charles R. Brown, USN.

the night that the Fanshaw Bay got bombed.* We put everything we had in the air and we drove them off, we shot down a lot, and Kelly Turner, who was the overall commander of the forces at Guam, asked me, "How many fighters have you got in the air?"*

So I said, "Forty-eight--every one that's in the four ships."

When the thing was all over, he sent me a message. He said, "You saved Saipan, and I'm very glad to congratulate you." Well, we didn't, but if he wanted to think that way, I wasn't going to disagree with him.

Q: Why do you say you didn't if he thought you did?

Admiral Bogan: Because I didn't think the threat was as bad as he seemed to think it was.

Q: What date was that now?

Admiral Bogan: I don't know. Very shortly after--it was in the latter part of June, not long after the operation started.

Q: Because I have what they called the "Marianas Turkey Shoot" as June 19th.

---

*The Fanshaw Bay (CVE-70) was hit by a Japanese bomb on 17 June 1944.
**Vice Admiral Richmond Kelly Turner, USN, Commander Task Force 51--Joint Expeditionary Force.

Admiral Bogan: That was the 19th and 20th, but that was the big fleet over to the west and southwest of Saipan. We operated east of Saipan.

Q: I see.

Admiral Bogan: The two had nothing to do with each other.

Q: But during that period of 14 June to 1 August, you received the Legion of Merit?

Admiral Bogan: Yes. I got the Legion of Merit.

Q: I'd like to read it. May I?

Admiral Bogan: I'll see if I can find it.

Q: I have it here. It says:

"For exceptionally meritorious conduct as commander of a carrier air support group engaged in operations for the capture of the Japanese-held southern Marianas Islands during the period 14 June to 1 August 1944. By his understanding, initiative, and outstanding ability, he conducted well coordinated bombing and strafing missions, antisubmarine and combat air patrols in support of the amphibious landing in this theater. His escort carriers were well organized and excellently handled. Their many aggressive missions contributed materially to the success of the operations."

Admiral Bogan: Well, that's a citation. There's an awful lot of crap in those things. You know that.

Q: No, but you only told me a little bit. You said one night the Japs . . .

Admiral Bogan: Well, that, I should say, was the one time when we really had what I would call a big aerial combat.

Q: How many Jap planes came over, did you say?

Admiral Bogan: I'd say there might have been 50 altogether.

Q: They came from Guam?

Admiral Bogan: They came from Guam, and Admiral Sallada had another division about 8 miles south of where my division was, and I was originally worried because the skipper of a tanker which was about 10 miles from us said, "I'm being attacked."*

---

*Rear Admiral Harold B. Sallada, USN, Commander Task Group 52.11.

Bogan #1 - 100

So I sent planes over, and before the Jap planes could dive on the tanker and set him afire, we knocked them both down. There were only two, and then the big group came in a little later. Now, none of these kids were night-qualified, and it was 8:00 or 9:00 o'clock that night when they began to come back, and I told them all to turn on their lights, and I turned the lights on on the flight deck, and some trigger-happy guy in one carrier or a screen destroyer, I don't know, shot down one of our own people as he was in the landing circle, and the last plane to land on the White Plains went through the barrier, wrecked 11 planes, and killed 11 people.

Q: Oh, no!

Admiral Bogan: Well, yes. So the next day, I sent Cat Brown and the Kalinin Bay back to Eniwetok to get more fighter planes, and as he went over the horizon, he sent me a message that said, "Do not engage the enemy until I return."

Q: Isn't that tragic?

Admiral Bogan: That was tragic, yes.

Q: Did you have to conduct a service for them the next day?

Admiral Bogan: I wasn't in the White Plains then; I was still on the Fanshaw Bay, but she'd been hit that night. I transferred the next morning.

Q: Tell me about the Fanshaw Bay being hit.

Admiral Bogan: Well, somebody shot him down afterwards, but he came in from the stern without a shot being fired at him, and he hit the after elevator. When the bomb exploded on the hangar deck, it killed the entire repair party there of 11 people and also broke the main fire main, a piece went through that. So I detached my operations officer as executive officer to replace the original executive officer who'd just left with diabetes or some other disease. I could feel this ship getting more and more unstable, so finally I told Pirie, who was chief of staff and who had commanded a similar ship, to go down there on the hangar deck and see what the hell was the matter. This ship was filling with water someplace. Well, just below the hangar deck was a storeroom about the size of this room, and this broken water main was pumping water into this thing. It was then 5 feet deep under 125-pound pressure, and they couldn't close the valve. Pirie, who was familiar with the thing, called the engine room and told them to shut off the pressure on the fire main, and when they did, he closed the valve, and that was that.

Q: But it was too late to save it?

Admiral Bogan: No, it wasn't too late to save it. She was just unstable, and during that night and the next morning, we tried to rig a siphon, and finally we emptied the damn thing out with buckets, so it was clear. But it was quite a lot of water, and it affected the stability of the ship, being above her metacentric height.

Q: Of course. And no one had been able to figure out what was wrong until he went down there?

Admiral Bogan: The entire repair party there had been killed by the explosion of this bomb, 11 men, and there was nobody there that seemed to know what to do. The skipper didn't seem to be interested. Nobody seemed to be interested, but I was, because it was my flagship and I didn't want to lose it. I told Pirie to go down, and in five minutes he saw the trouble and had the pressure taken off and was able to close the gate valve. You can't close the valve with 125 pounds of pressure against you.

Q: But the next day, you transferred then to the White Plains?

Admiral Bogan: Yes. The Fanshaw Bay went back first to Eniwetok, then to Pearl for repairs. The funny part of it was I was invited to go to Washington from Norfolk to participate in a group of presidential citations being given to these former ships, one of which was the Fanshaw Bay. I didn't attend. I didn't want to see Mr. Truman, and I didn't want to be a hypocrite to be there while that ship got a Presidential Unit Citation.*

Q: Now, I have another comment here that, at the beginning of the campaign, the CVEs of the expeditionary force under the command of Rear Admiral Bogan, Sallada, and Stump maintained, from dawn to dusk, fighters and bombers orbiting two air stations 8 miles offshore to deliver, when called for, strikes promptly, which was a new wrinkle in amphibious warfare.**

Admiral Bogan: That's correct, but Sallada and Stump--Sallada was there for a few days. He was originally scheduled to support the Guam operation, which was postponed because of the length of time that Saipan took. He happened to be with us the day that these Japs came over, but, as I told you, I never saw Stump at all in that operation.

Q: Oh, really? It was your division?

---
*Harry S. Truman, President from April 1945 to January 1953.
**Rear Admiral Felix B. Stump, USN, Commander Carrier Division 24.

Bogan #1 - 104

Admiral Bogan: My division and, with Sallada's assistance that day, we had the big attack.

Q: Was that at night, you said?

Admiral Bogan: Oh, they came over about 5:00 o'clock, and it was dark at 6:30, and we began to land them at around 8:00.

Q: By the time they got back, it was dark. Then you went to Saipan, back to Ulithi?

Admiral Bogan: Back to Eniwetok--this was before Ulithi--and shifted to Task Force 58 and went aboard the Essex as my flagship. That task group provided the air support for Guam, which was not nearly as demanding or as long as Saipan. In other words, the Japs at Guam were hidden, and the Marines were having trouble locating them, so they didn't call for as much air support as they had in Saipan, which is more open country.

Q: And you were on the Essex by this time?

Admiral Bogan: Yes.

Q: And what ships were with you at that time?

Admiral Bogan: I can't remember the names. There was a division of battleships. Admiral Lee had command of them; as a matter of fact, he had all the battleships in Task Force 58.* He just happened to be in my group. A division of cruisers, and there were several destroyers. I believe there was one other carrier whose name I've forgotten now, and two CVLs of the Independence class.

Q: And how long were you off Guam?

Admiral Bogan: I'd say two and a half to three weeks. No more.

Q: By the time you left, Guam was secured?

Admiral Bogan: Yes. It had been secured a couple of days before we left.

Q: And then where did you go?

Admiral Bogan: Then we went back to Eniwetok, and Task Force 58, as a unit, began a sweep that took us well to the southwest and up to the Philippines.

---

*Vice Admiral Willis A. Lee, Jr., USN, Commander Battleships Pacific Fleet.

Bogan #1 - 106

Q: In October, did you go into the China Sea?

Admiral Bogan: No, that was the following January.

Q: I have a note that on 12 October an attack on Formosa from four carrier groups made 10,378 sorties. The Franklin was hit and also the Canberra, but that was in October.

Admiral Bogan: The Franklin was in Davison's group.* I don't know where the Canberra was. I think that was the second time we hit Formosa, and they were ready for us. The first time was a complete surprise.

Q: When was the first attack against Formosa?

Admiral Bogan: I can't remember the dates at this time, but I believe the 12th of October was the second one, because that's when the Japs came out and we had the first evidence of the kamikaze. They hit, not the Canberra, but the Belleau Wood and the Franklin, and the following night, about 5:00 o'clock, the Houston, which had sustained another torpedo attack, and she was eventually towed back into Ulithi, which was opened by that time. The Japanese had these wide press releases that they'd sunk the

---
*Rear Admiral Ralph E. Davison, USN, Commander Task Group 38.4.

entire carrier fleet, and Halsey sent a message that the carrier fleet was now retreating in the direction of Japan. A light cruiser, the Reno, either torpedoed or hit a mine, was commanded by R.C. Alexander, but we weren't there.* We were still up off Okinawa or someplace up in there, while this group went down to-- the damaged ships eventually reached Ulithi and safety. At that time, we'd stay on the line in an area 33 or 34 days, go back to Ulithi for four days for refueling and reprovisioning, and then go out again. That was before the Sixth Squadron which tankered, mobile tankered, the last two operations--Okinawa was 87 days and the last one from the 30th of June until the end of the war, but we never got there. We went ashore then.

Q: After Formosa came the Battle of the Philippine Sea, didn't it?

Admiral Bogan: Well, they called it the Battle of Leyte Gulf. First of all, the Second Battle of the Philippine Sea, and then MacArthur insisted it be called the Battle of Leyte Gulf.**

Q: What ship were you on then? I know you were 38.2.

---

*On 3 November 1944, the USS Reno (CL-96), commanded by Captain Ralph C. Alexander, USN, was torpedoed by the Japanese submarine I-41.
**General Douglas MacArthur, USA, Supreme Commander Allied Forces Southwest Pacific Area.

Admiral Bogan: I was in the Intrepid.

Q: Can you describe that whole action for me, because that is of great interest?

Admiral Bogan: We were off--four groups, Sherman and the Lexington, 38.3, was up north.* Davison was well south, and McCain had just started back to Ulithi to refuel and resupply.** We sent this scouting force, armed scouting force, to the west about 7:30 in the morning, and about 9:30 saw this central force under Admiral Kurita which had already lost two cruisers to submarines, the Dace and the Darter, the day before off Palawan.*** Then Davison was called north, although he didn't join in time, and my group made several attacks throughout the day, as this central force came back and around through the Sibuyan Sea. Admiral Sherman's group, 38.3, also sent one very heavy attack at about 3:00 o'clock, and I don't know whether it was as a result of that or cumulative effects from previous attacks, which caused the Musashi, a sister ship of the Yamato, to slow down, and the rest of the force then turned around for a few minutes to cover her. Halsey got that report and thought

---

*Rear Admiral Frederick C. Sherman, USN, Commander Task Group 38.3.
**Vice Admiral John S. McCain, USN, Commander Task Group 38.1.
***Vice Admiral Takeo Kurita, IJN, Commander First Striking Force. The times referred to were on 24 October 1944.

they were retreating. In my group was the Independence, which carried a night group, and we kept surveillance over the central force until about 11:00 o'clock, when we were too far away to do it anymore. Meantime, Halsey had ordered all three groups, Davison, Sherman, and myself, north at 25 knots to attack what turned out to be a decoy force. There were 17 ships in it, and we had 68. I then talked to Captain Ewen in the Independence, and he said that they were on a course of 060°, and were coming out through San Bernardino Strait, and navigation lights in the strait were turned on for the first time.* I thought that Admiral Halsey was making one hell of a mistake. I had this message all ready to send him saying, "Recommend Form Leo [which was Task Force 34]. Leave my group in support and let the other two groups handle the northern force."** But when I told him about the light business, somebody on his staff said, "Yes, yes, we have that information." That was a brushoff, as far as I was concerned, and I wasn't going to say any more. I doubt very much if it would have had any effect, because Admiral Halsey talked to me time after time and justified his decision to go north. Arleigh Burke, Mitscher's chief of staff, tried to get him to recommend something to Halsey, but Mitscher, who felt the

---

*Captain Edward C. Ewen, USN.
**Task Force 34 would have comprised Vice Admiral Lee's fast battleships. There had been a tentative plan for them to stay behind to counter Kurita's heavy ships, but it was not implemented.

tactical command had been taken away from him, said, "If he wants plans or information from me, he'll ask for it."* He did nothing.

Then about 2:00 o'clock in the morning, Admiral Halsey ordered a search made from the Independence in my group for these ships.** Admiral Mitscher protested, saying he thought that if the planes got up in the air, the Japanese radar would discover them and change course. Halsey said, "Launch the search." The search was launched, the Japs did discover them in the air, and did change course, and instead of this gun duel which Halsey had envisioned early in the morning, it was nearly 8:30 before we could even catch them with planes. And about 10:30, after the second strike, when the thing was practically over, we had sunk all three carriers. Admiral Nimitz sent this message to Admiral Halsey, "Where is Task Force 34?" And there was a little padding on the end which some kid put on, "All the world wants to know."

And that just turned Halsey on his ear. "God, why is Nimitz sending me a message like that?"*** So, at 11:30, we formed Task Force 34 with my group in support and started back to the Philippines at full 28 knots, refueling destroyers at 14 knots until they were filled. Of course, Kurita had knocked off the

---

*Commodore Arleigh A. Burke, USN, chief of staff to Vice Admiral Marc A. Mitscher, USN, Commander Task Force 38.
**This occurred the morning of 25 October 1944.
***Admiral Chester W. Nimitz, USN, Commander in Chief Pacific Fleet.

action about noon and had gone west again, after suffering pretty heavy losses, and nobody ever knew why he turned around, but he did. He'd sunk four little jeep carriers and two destroyers, and had he continued he could have wiped out the landing force at Leyte Gulf. Nobody's ever known why he turned around.

Q: Miraculous that he did.

Admiral Bogan: Yes, it is. And nobody--even in his book, it's right over there, <u>Admiral Halsey's Story</u>--he justified that decision to me.* He had the jackpot in his hand and he paid off at three to one.

Q: And you say that he justified it to you. How did he try to justify it to you?

Admiral Bogan: Well, he said, "I thought that was Kinkaid's responsibility to guard that strait, not mine."** It's a long story and it will never be resolved, except that I'm clear in my own mind that it was a great mistake on Halsey's part.

Q: Well, one of the problems, as I read the books, was that

---
*Fleet Admiral William F. Halsey, USN, and Lieutenant Commander Joseph Bryan III, USNR, <u>Admiral Halsey's Story</u> (New York: Whittlesey House, 1947).
**Vice Admiral Thomas C. Kinkaid, USN, Commander Seventh Fleet.

between the Seventh Fleet, Kinkaid, and between Halsey, there was no direct communication.

Admiral Bogan: Also there was no direct chain of command. Halsey had orders to aggressively support the landings at Leyte, and here was a big force coming through which was about to destroy those landings and he did not provide support. And also, while Kinkaid had launched aircraft searchers that morning, he had left open a sector which was not searched, through which Kurita had come, and he didn't see him until there they were astern of all these little carriers.

Q: Had they been in communication, they would have undoubtedly recognized that there was an area that wasn't covered.

Admiral Bogan: Kinkaid misinterpreted a dispatch from Halsey, a dispatch that said, "Be prepared to form Task Force 34." And Kinkaid assumed that Task Force 34 had been formed, which, of course, it wasn't because it was a preparatory message, not an executive message.

Q: And he never did send an executive?

Admiral Bogan: No. In other words, I wanted to form it the night before--we were going north--and come back and stay out there with my task group in support, and let the six battleships and the cruisers, Task Force 34, handle these Japs coming through. It could have been a slaughter. It could have meant the end of Japanese naval power right there. Completely.

Q: How did that make you feel? When you know something in your own mind is right and it doesn't happen, doesn't get accomplished?

Admiral Bogan: It's hard for me to put myself in your place, but I felt that some girl had said yes, and I wasn't ready.

Q: That's hardly the answer I expected you to give.

Admiral Bogan: I know, but that's the answer.

Q: Well, I'll accept that. But I'm sure it must have been extremely frustrating.

Admiral Bogan: Oh, it was. Eddie Outlaw, Bob Pirie, and I discussed this thing for 45 minutes, because I didn't think that the message that Eddie Ewen, the skipper of the Independence, sent out was sufficiently strong to alarm Halsey to all the implications.* I called Eddie on the TBS myself, just as you and I are sitting here, and he said, "Yes. They're on course 060°, navigational lights are on, they're coming out through San Bernardino Strait."** One of Halsey's justifications was that he overestimated the reports of damage that the pilots made on this force during the afternoon of the 24th. Well, unless you're right there and see the picture, you don't know. You can only tell how many hits you've made, and you don't know how strong the ships are, what they can take. Anyway, he died thinking he did the right thing.

Q: Then, when you came south, you still stayed around the Philippines for some time. Can you describe your operations then?

Admiral Bogan: They were really nothing. McCain had been called back, and his group made one long-distance strike against the retreating Kurita force, but inflicted no damage, and then he went on to Ulithi, and then Sherman and Davison went back to Ulithi, and my group was left there alone for, maybe, two weeks until they got back. Admiral Halsey was in the New Jersey and was in my group. He was only 1,500 yards from me. So the top

---
*Commander Edward C. Outlaw, USN. The message from the Independence had warned that Admiral Kurita's force was headed east toward San Bernardino Strait. Thus, it posed a threat to the amphibious and support forces in Leyte Gulf.
**TBS--talk between ships, voice radio.

commander was right there, but my group was the only one for the next two weeks.

Q: And tell me what your operations were.

Admiral Bogan: Well, they were just routine bombing in support of the Leyte operations and a few strikes against, I've forgotten whether we went up as far as Manila or not, but I think we probably did. We were in and out of there all the time. It was just routine. There was nothing to distinguish it from what had gone before, except a smaller force because there was only one group.

Q: Was this about the time when the first kamikaze strikes had happened?

Admiral Bogan: The first kamikazes were the ones that hit the Franklin and the Belleau Wood.

Q: Was that up on the attack on Formosa?

Admiral Bogan: Yes. Maybe it was off the Philippines. I'm not sure. Then on the 25th of November, the Intrepid took a kamikaze on the gun gallery which killed 11 men and a 20-millimeter gun crew. It did not damage. Then, two weeks after that, we got two kamikazes that were really bad. The first one dived right on the flight deck, and the second one almost came in as if it were making a carrier landing, and you could see the imprint of its wings on the deck, and the engine and the pilot rolled up the deck, and the bomb exploded on the hangar deck. We had a very tough time for about two hours in the Intrepid controlling that fire. I got the Navy Cross for that.

Q: For the second one?

Admiral Bogan: For the kamikazes in the Intrepid, yes. And she went back to Ulithi.

Q: I have that day as November 25th for your Navy Cross.

Admiral Bogan: That's what I said. It was the 25th when these kamikazes hit us.

Q: Oh, I see. Yes, okay. I misunderstood.

Admiral Bogan: One thing happened that day that I would like to give credit to my ACI officer, a man named Ben Sturges, who comes from Providence, Rhode Island.* The reason the damage to the

---

*Lieutenant Benjamin R. Sturges, USNR. ACI--air combat intelligence.

Intrepid was not greater was that one strike had been launched and had been out about two hours, and we had just finished launching the other strike, so there were only 17 planes aboard on the hangar deck. And Admiral McCain, who was then commander of the force, said, "Well, when these planes come back, we'll land them on the Hancock, the flagship, take the pilots off and throw the planes over the side." That was about $4 million worth of airplanes, and little Sturges, who was my ACI officer, said, "Well, they're over near the Philippines now. Don't you think they could land at Tacloban?" which was the new field there at Leyte.

I said, "That's a hell of a good idea. Let's do it." So I called McCain, and Wilder Baker was his chief of staff.* My communications had been burned up so I couldn't talk to the planes, but I still had command of the task group. So I said, "Tell those planes to land at Tacloban instead of trying to return to the task group."

He said, "The field isn't ready."

I said, "There are over 100 Army airplanes on it right now. Tell them to land there and don't give me any argument about it."

Baker said, "This is your boss's chief of staff."

So I said, "I'm commanding this task group. Tell them to land there." So they did, and four days later they flew from

---
*Rear Admiral Wilder D. Baker, USN.

Tacloban to Palau, then to Yap, with a seaplane escort of Mariners, and then Ulithi. And all the planes were there and able to be used again, and the pilots with the group. Nobody was lost, and the <u>Intrepid</u> went back to Hunters Point to repair, and I shifted to the <u>Lexington</u>, and I got the kid a Bronze Star for it, which I think he deserved.* Four million bucks of planes just thrown over the side unnecessarily, even in wartime, I'd call tragic.

Q: If it isn't necessary. Does that make you remember back to the days when you had trouble with flying back at Pensacola, McCain?

Admiral Bogan: I've got to say it does. Pete Mitscher, in my opinion made over the years, was a consummate master of naval air power, and when he ran Task Force 58 or 38, whichever you call it, it was a professional outfit, doing a professional job, in a professional way. When McCain ran it, it was a goddamn circus. He'd come up with one screwy idea after another. One night we changed the bomb load on the planes three times for morning strikes. Now, those kids had been working 24 hours on the flight deck, and when you have to change a load of bombs on 47 planes three times during the night, that's not . . .

---

*Hunters Point was the site of the San Francisco Navy Yard.

Bogan #1 - 119

Q: What was the occasion for that?

Admiral Bogan: Just an idea he had, that different bombs might be better on the targets we were going to hit. It was just--well, it was disgusting to me, and there was nothing you could do about it. But he went on in a big way and he came back here to Coronado and died of heart failure.* I got a letter from him before he left at the end of the war.

Q: I'd like to read your citation for the Navy Cross, and then I'd like to have you enlarge on the experience of that day. It says:

"For extraordinary heroism as Commander Task Group 38.2 during operations against enemy Japanese forces, November 25, 1944, when all the carriers under his command were damaged by enemy aerial attack, including two bomb hits on his own flagship, Rear Admiral Bogan continued to fight his forces so vigorously that eight enemy aircraft were shot down by his ships' gunfire and the remaining enemy aircraft flew away. By his courage and leadership, he contributed directly to the success of our forces in this area."

Can't you describe that day to me?

---

*Vice Admiral McCain died on 6 September 1945, four days after the Japanese surrender on board the USS Missouri (BB-63).

Admiral Bogan: Yes, I can. In naval hero Clark's book you will see that because he had the best group he was always closest to the land targets.* It just happens that 38.2 was usually closest to the land targets and we were closest that day, and several groups--Japanese groups--had followed our own planes back towards the task force. Sherman's group was to the north of us, and they were engaging some, and then suddenly these 18 planes appeared from someplace, and Sherman said, "I can handle them, too." And the next thing we knew, about ten minutes later, here were these 18 planes over 38.2. One dived on the New Jersey, which was Halsey's flagship, and they had the best antiaircraft batteries in the fleet, in the world, at that time. They knocked it down. And two planes came in about 600 feet and passed over the Iowa, which was Oscar Badger's flagship.** They shot one down, and it landed in the ocean, a mass of flames. This other one had a slight flame on one wing, but instead of shifting to that one, the Iowa with all these antiaircraft guns, kept firing at this flaming mass in the water. The one that was on fire came up, and we were shooting at it with 40-millimeters and 20-millimeters, which was all we had at that range, and we didn't hit him. And when he was about 400 feet off the starboard bow, he did the wingover and dived right into the center of the flight deck, just

---
*Admiral Joseph J. Clark, USN(Ret.), with Clark G. Reynolds, Carrier Admiral (New York: David McKay Company, Inc., 1967).
**Rear Admiral Oscar C. Badger, USN, Commander Battleship Division Seven.

before the flag room. Well, he had a big bomb that created a hell of a lot of damage in the area under the flight deck, smoke mostly. And then, while this whole thing was obscured by smoke, just a few minutes later, this other one just came in as if he were making a carrier landing, and landed in the arresting gear, nose down, and his bomb exploded in the hangar deck. The body of the pilot and the engine rolled all the way forward and stopped near the bow. A few minutes later, I was down there, I saw this Jap pilot, and I said to this kid who was standing there, "At Guadalcanal I understand the Marines used to knock out their teeth and get the gold."

He reached in his pocket and he said, "I heard about that, too. Here they are."

Q: The Jap was dead, of course?

Admiral Bogan: Oh, sure, he was dead. So we had it under control in about, I'd say, two hours, went back to Ulithi, and I told you how the air group got back, and then the _Intrepid_ went back to Hunters Point for repairs, and came out again.

Q: You make it sound easy.

Admiral Bogan: On Christmas Day I was over in the _New Jersey_ for Christmas dinner in Admiral Halsey's flagship, and they had a colored moving picture of this whole thing, which, of course, I didn't know they had. Admiral Nimitz was there. After the attack, Joe Bolger, who was skipper of the Intrepid, would say, "Will you make a hard right turn, so that the ship will heel to port and this gasoline will go overside."*

This picture taken from the New Jersey as we made the turns, this water and gasoline just went over the side. It was a solid sheet of red. During the course of this picture, Admiral Halsey said, "Jerry, did it look like that to you?"

And I said, "It was quite a bit closer, but it wasn't this colorful."

Q: Could you have got the effect of it when it was happening? Could you recognize . . ?

Admiral Bogan: No, you see I was on the starboard side, on the island, and we'd make these turns to starboard, so the ship would heel to port and everything went out the port side, so I saw nothing of it.

Q: Where were you when the first kamikaze hit?

Admiral Bogan: On the flag bridge.

---

*Captain Joseph F. Bolger, USN.

Bogan #1 - 123

Q: And you saw it coming in?

Admiral Bogan: I saw it coming in, because I think that if the *Iowa* had shifted from the plane that was already shot down to this thing, with the volume of antiaircraft fire, it wouldn't have hit.

Q: Yes. Then you went back to Ulithi, and that ended, what, about 84 days of . . ?

Admiral Bogan: It was a long time. I can't remember it.

Q: I think the books say 84 days that you were . . .

Admiral Bogan: And then we shifted to the *Lexington*, which had just completed repairs after having hit by a kamikaze on the starboard flag bridge about a month before.

Q: And you were at sea almost continuously for 84 days. And for that you had another Distinguished Service Medal.

Admiral Bogan: I got two of them.

Q: The first one was for 30 October 1944 to 25 January 1945, and that was when you, according to the citation, were commander of the task group assigned to duty with the Second Carrier Task Force of the Pacific Fleet.

Admiral Bogan: That's right.

Q: From 30 October to 25 January 1945. "Under his direction, his task group completed highly successful operations against enemy aircraft, shipping, and land installations in the Philippine Islands, Formosa, and the Nansei Shoto Islands, and the coast of Indochina. His ability to organize, direct, and inspire the forces under his command to their maximum effort resulted in devastating damage being inflicted on the enemy."

Interview Number 2 with Vice Admiral Gerald F. Bogan,
U.S. Navy (Retired)

Place: Admiral Bogan's home in La Jolla, California

Date: 26 October 1969

Subject: Biography

Interviewer: Commander Etta-Belle Kitchen, U.S. Navy (Retired)

Admiral Bogan: In the Lexington we went back, oh, about the first of December, to the Philippines again. Then on the 18th of December, we got caught in this typhoon, which we never should have been caught in. I asked Admiral Halsey not to take the course that he was taking. The weather station at Guam and my own meteorologists had said differently. But he had a date to support MacArthur two days later in the Philippines, and with the course the typhoon was taking, the weather would have been such that we couldn't have operated anyway. So I suggested he steer south, which he did for a few hours, and then came back and got on the same course he had been on. I'd left one of my destroyers, which McCain wouldn't let me finish fueling, with the oiler group, the tenth, and the Spence, and Hull, and the Monaghan were lost with 805 men, which was just something. I couldn't live with that on my conscience. That was it. We spent

Christmas week in Ulithi.

Q: Where were you during this typhoon?

Admiral Bogan: In the Lexington.

Q: I mean, where was the Lexington? Were you in the typhoon?

Admiral Bogan: Yes, we were in the typhoon, but these destroyers that were low on fuel were just being capsized by the sea. The fueling group was several miles away from us, but they were in the general area, and they lost these three cans and 805 men.*

Q: How far away were they from you? A mile?

Admiral Bogan: Oh, no. Maybe 50 miles. We spent the next few days in searching the area, but I don't think we picked up more than ten people out of those four boats.

Q: How did you feel then?

Admiral Bogan: I felt that it was just plain, goddamn stubbornness and stupidity. All the information was available

---

*"Can" or "tincan" is a slang term for a destroyer.

that this area we went to was going to be the heart of the typhoon, and the further information was that the direction it was moving would prevent any strikes Admiral Halsey felt he had to make against the Philippines two days later. In other words, we'd be over there with no ceiling and heavy storms.

Q: And here you've had two incidents of Admiral Halsey making, in your opinion, real bad decisions.

Admiral Bogan: Yes, but he didn't think so.

Q: Didn't he, even at the time of the typhoon, even take responsibility for that?

Admiral Bogan: Well, there was nobody else to take responsibility.

Q: No, I mean didn't he feel bad or think he'd made a mistake?

Admiral Bogan: I don't know. I couldn't ask him.

Q: You can't tell. And how did you react to it, when you're under the command of a man . . .

Admiral Bogan: I thought it was a needless, tragic loss of life and material.

Q: Nothing you could do about it, though?

Admiral Bogan: Nothing. I'd done all I could in recommending that he not go where he did.

Q: On both occasions?

Admiral Bogan: Yes, and at a court of inquiry later, they asked me, "Did you make any recommendations to Admiral Halsey about the course that he steered?"

And I had the copy of the message right with me, and I said, "There it is."

Q: I wanted to go back to your service. We talked about 25 November, and then you said Christmas Day you were in the New Jersey.

Admiral Bogan: We were anchored in Ulithi, and I went over for Christmas dinner in the New Jersey with Admiral Halsey, and they showed a picture of the Intrepid after the kamikaze hit, in color. It was very brilliant and very well done. Admiral Halsey said to me, "Did it look like this to you?"

And I said, "No, I'm sorry it wasn't as colorful from where I sat."

Q: You were too busy also, I'm sure.

Admiral Bogan: Yes. We were very busy. Then after Christmas, we went over to the Philippines and from the eastern side supported the landings in Lingayen Gulf; General MacArthur was landing in the north on the island of Luzon. And after a few days there, we snaked through the Babuyan Island Straits north of Luzon, and went into the China Sea.

Q: Where are the Nansei?

Admiral Bogan: Shoto Islands.

Q: You pointed them out as being off the coast of southeast China.

Admiral Bogan: Yes. I think Hainan is one and there are others between Hong Kong and Hainan. They don't show on this map.

Q: And you reached them by going through the strait between Luzon and Formosa?

Admiral Bogan: That's correct.

Q: And did you operate along the coast of Indochina?

Admiral Bogan: We had quite a field day intercepting and sinking convoys, destroying a great many planes, and one French cruiser captured by the Japs at Saigon, drove several ships ashore in Camranh Bay, and sank two cruisers. The Japanese reinforced Saigon that evening with about 27 Betty aircraft, which a strike from our night group in the *Independence* completely destroyed on the ground at the airfield at Saigon. Then we swung north and after two days of bombing of Hong Kong and the islands nearby, came back through the strait between Taiwan and Luzon, and again attacked Formosa.

Q: When did that action end? That was about the 25th of January?

Admiral Bogan: No, it was earlier. The early part of January. I would say between the seventh and the 12th.

Q: And then you went back to Ulithi after that?

Admiral Bogan: Eventually we went back to Ulithi, and I went on leave on the 25th of January before the first Tokyo raid.

Q: Where did you go on leave?

Bogan #2 - 131

Admiral Bogan: Came back to Pearl Harbor and stayed there for a few days while Bob Pirie and I arranged for some decorations for the air group in the strike and the staff, and then flew to San Francisco and went down to Santa Barbara.

Q: Was that the first leave you'd had since you started operating in the Pacific?

Admiral Bogan: The first in about 20 months, I guess. At the conclusion of my leave, I took six enlisted men who had not been in the Pacific very long and five officers back with me, and left the rest of the staff to remain for their full period of leave and return by sea, rather than by air. We flew from Pearl Harbor to Guam, Guam to Ulithi, with orders to report on board the Randolph. However, on arrival at Ulithi, we found that the Randolph had been hit by a kamikaze the night before while at anchor, and was severely damaged in the after end of the flight deck.* So instead we went to the Franklin. Davison was already aboard the Franklin, and we sailed two days later for the assault on Kyushu preparatory to the opening of the Okinawa campaign. I believe the Essex was hit by a bomb or a kamikaze the first day, but we escaped any serious attack. However, on the morning of the 19th of March, at about five minutes after 7:00, Hancock, a

---

*The kamikaze hit on the Randolph (CV-15) took place on 11 March 1945.

carrier in this group, reported a bogey bearing 355°, distance 10 miles.* My status was that of a passenger, but out of curiosity I went to a porthole in flag ops and, in about two minutes, a Jap flew out between holes in a cloud barrier at 2,200 feet and over the deck at about an altitude of 200 feet and dropped two 500-pound bombs. The flight deck was loaded with planes in the process of taking off, fully armed, and the force of the explosions threw them on their backs or off their landing gear so that they could not be moved to salvage or jettison, and in a very few minutes the forward part of the ship was an inferno. My fighter director officer, Jim Winston, who was, in my opinion, the best in the fleet, was in the combat information center of the Franklin instructing his less experienced contemporaries.** The forward bomb blew everything in CIC to pieces, and it came through the flight deck, right through the flag officer's quarters forward. The only reason I'm alive today is that I'd been sleeping there and the previous morning I had slept until 8:00 o'clock. This morning I awoke at 4:30 and decided to go to the bridge to see what kind of a show Davison ran. The explosion also tore out the athwartship passageway back of flag quarters which led to a ladder to the hangar deck, and when I got aboard the Franklin, two days later at Ulithi, there were 14 people

---
*A "bogey" is an unidentified air contact.
**Lieutenant Commander Francis Lloyd Winston, USN, a member of Admiral Bogan's Carrier Division Four staff, was killed on board the Franklin (CV-13) on 19 March 1945.

piled against an exit door that led out to the gallery deck, just below the flight deck. In the smoke they had been unable to find the dog to undog the door so that they could get out, and some of them had their fingers worn down to the first knuckle, they'd scraped to get this door open.

Q: What a terrible, terrible experience.

Admiral Bogan: And I think that the ship's crew did a very fine job in fighting the thing, marked especially by the efforts of the chaplain, Joe O'Callahan, who later received the Medal of Honor for his effort that morning.* When we left to go to the Hancock or the Wasp . . .

Q: Didn't one of the doctors die, also because of his attempt to go down in the smoke and bring men up?

Admiral Bogan: That was in the Intrepid.

Q: That was in the Intrepid rather than the Franklin.

Admiral Bogan: I would say the fire was under control when we shifted to the Wasp around 10:30, but around 11:00 o'clock the

---

*Lieutenant Commander Joseph O'Callahan, CHC, USNR.

smoke in the firerooms became so great that they had to abandon the firerooms and therefore the ship lost power. Water to fight the fire was fortunately provided by an emergency motor generator and pump on the hangar deck which gave adequate streams of water forward.

Q: Did they use foam in those days?

Admiral Bogan: Not then. A couple of months later, they had it, but not then. And at about 1:00 o'clock that afternoon, the Pittsburgh took Franklin in tow and started to get her clear of the area. At 10:00 o'clock that night, the fires being out, they were able to light off a couple of boilers, and by midnight she was making 20 knots, which she did all the way back to Ulithi.

Q: How many lives were lost on the Franklin?

Admiral Bogan: I think 840. The next morning I got a destroyer to take me around to the various ships and the various other destroyers in this new task group that was . . .

Q: Where had you spent the night?

Admiral Bogan: I spent the night on the Hancock. And picked up several members of my staff and Davison's staff, who had either been blown over the side or jumped over the side when they had to to escape the flames. After we left the Franklin, the Santa Fe came alongside on the starboard side and assisted materially in fighting fires and was a great help in extinguishing them. I noticed one thing--that the first time the ship was hit, the entire crew was very outgoing in fighting the flames and the damage, and later on when they began to think about it, they begin to imagine things. Now, this was the second time the Franklin had been hit, although not as seriously the first time. And there were all sorts of conduct, from sheer heroism--which is a word I don't like--to abject panic and cowardice.

Q: Can you give me instances for both of those?

Admiral Bogan: The officers' quarters forward had a little corrugated steel bulkhead. A good many of the crew, in an effort to escape the flames, went through the officers' quarters. They broke open the safes, they robbed them, and one chief of the Santa Fe was found with $300 in bills stuck up his rectum, which he'd stolen from officers' quarters.

Q: You're kidding!

Admiral Bogan: I'm not kidding.

Q: Of course you're not because you wouldn't say it.

Admiral Bogan: They also found one seaman in a commander's uniform. That was one group. Those were the weaklings. The other people did their job until it was over.

Q: Were you ever scared?

Admiral Bogan: One always wonders before the first action what one's reactions were going to be, and I found out that I was so busy doing my job I never had a chance to think about myself. In Christmas week of 1944 in Ulithi, away from the war and in my bunk one night while the ship was anchored, no danger, I just got the shakes that lasted for about half an hour. I just had uncontrollable shakes. Now, it wasn't fear; it was just nervous spasms.

Q: Well, I'm sure you'd been so terribly keyed up from the experience back in November, it was a delayed reaction, when you weren't under stress.

Admiral Bogan: But that's the only time that I ever felt the least loss of control. And it wasn't worry then; it was just nervous spasms that I could not control nor understand.

Q: That probably startled you more than anything else, that you were having a physical reaction that you couldn't control.

Admiral Bogan: That's right. It did.

Q: What was the ship that was anchored in Leyte Gulf when one of its own planes came over and . . .

Admiral Bogan: That was not one of its own planes. It was an Army P-38 camera plane.

We had just taken Admiral Mitscher to Guam and come back to Leyte. The Okinawa campaign was about over, and I had left this exercise room under the forward part of the flight deck and saw this Army plane dive out of the west and pass over the ship at about 200 feet. He climbed again, made another dive, and this time he pulled out so rapidly he squashed. One blade of the propeller hit the flight deck, the plane hit the bow of the flight deck, and he bounced over the side. There were a great many planes parked at the bow. They caught fire. There were groups of crew sunning themselves there and I think 17 planes were burned up and 14 people killed by flat-hatting by this pilot. Of course, he was killed, too, but I didn't waste any sympathy on him.

Q: What was the carrier?

Admiral Bogan: The Randolph.

Q: You've been on so many carriers, unless you specifically identify them it's hard to know where you were when what happened.

Admiral Bogan: I spent the last five months of the war in the Randolph, and came back to Pearl. Then she was ordered to the East Coast immediately on this Magic Carpet thing to bring the boys home to Mama.*

Q: But I don't want to get ahead of your story. We were at . . .

Admiral Bogan: Leaving the Franklin, I guess.

Q: On leaving the Franklin, you spent the night on the Hancock, and the next day picked up some of your staff . . .

Admiral Bogan: . . . the staff and went back to Ulithi in the Hancock. There we waited for a few days for the Randolph's repairs to be completed and, acting under radio-telegraphic orders from Admiral Halsey, I took a small group of new ships

---

*During the postwar Magic Carpet operation, combatant ships were used as transports.

that were in Ulithi out for five days' training before rejoining Task Force 38.

Q: What kind of ships?

Admiral Bogan: Destroyers and a cruiser division and, I believe, one CVL. I've forgotten now. It was just a conglomeration.

Q: I see. They were varied.

Admiral Bogan: Yes. We formed a little task group for training purposes, just were outside Ulithi for about a week. Then we rejoined Task Force 38 and operated off Okinawa and after about a week of that due, not to damages to my own ship, but damages to ships in other groups, Task Group 38.2 was dissolved and the ships distributed in the other groups. So I was just riding as a passenger from then on in the Randolph in Admiral Sherman's group until the end of the Okinawa campaign.

Q: And for how long? What was that date when that finished?

Admiral Bogan: That date would be about the eighth of June, I think. I was about seven weeks as a passenger.

Q: In 1945?

Bogan #2 - 140

Admiral Bogan: Yes.

Q: What happened during that time? What did you do when you were a passenger? Observe?

Admiral Bogan: Well, partially, but Admiral Mitscher was bombed out of the Bunker Hill, and he shifted to the Enterprise, and after about a week in the Enterprise, she was bombed, and her elevator was knocked askew, fairly heavy fire damage, so Admiral Mitscher joined me in the Randolph. He had lost some of his staff in these two bombing attacks, so I offered him the use of my staff while he was there, and he ran the show, Task Force 38, from the Randolph until he was relieved about a week before the end of the campaign by Admiral McCain, who was then in the Hancock, I believe.

Q: Did he give you any duties to perform?

Admiral Bogan: No, not during that time. Sherman was running the task group, and Mitscher was running the whole task force.

Q: So there was no need for you to do . . .

Admiral Bogan: It wasn't particularly severe with the fast carriers where we were on the eastern side of Okinawa, but the landing forces and the picket destroyers on the western side were subjected to savage kamikaze attacks, and I think 55 ships were sunk or damaged there, in that area. So when Mitscher was relieved by McCain, we took him to Guam, left him and the nucleus of his staff there, and returned to Leyte Gulf.

Q: You had great regard for Mitscher, didn't you?

Admiral Bogan: I know of no finer man, personally or professionally.

Q: And Arleigh Burke was his chief of staff?

Admiral Bogan: Arleigh was his chief of staff, yes. Arleigh's a very forthright person and a very fine person.

Q: A colorful man, too.

Admiral Bogan: Yes, he is. Shortly after we got to Leyte, the force which had been off Okinawa assembled at Leyte Gulf, and I was ordered to take Task Group 38.3 and relieve Fred Sherman, who had been previous commander of that group. Admiral Halsey sent me out for a week outside Leyte for training exercises with the Bonhomme Richard, which had a night flyer group aboard, and on the 30th of June we sailed for Japan.

Q: Had the Bonhomme Richard just come . . .

Admiral Bogan: She had newly arrived, and she was not in my group, but she was in Radford's group during that last operation.*

Q: I wondered how you got from 38.2 to 38.3.

Admiral Bogan: That was it.

Q: I see now.

Admiral Bogan: Sherman had had 38.3, and 38.2 had been dissolved. The Okinawa campaign was the last straw as far as the Japanese were concerned. The last cruise off the coast of Japan from the last of June until the surrender was more or less anticlimax. We had opposition but nothing we couldn't handle. I don't know of any ships that were damaged, and we were sometimes at a loss to find adequate targets in Japan, because they had camouflaged and covered up and hidden their few remaining planes on the ground and under trees and under leaves. So it took, first, a photographic reconnaissance to discover those things, and then a strike to hit them. We did have two days, I believe,

---
*Rear Admiral Arthur W. Radford, USN, Commander Task Group 38.4.

of hitting Kure naval base, which was very rewarding in destroying the rest of the Japanese Navy.

Q: Can you clarify for me the period of time in which Task Group 38 went into the China Sea and wreaked such havoc with the Japanese fleet?

Admiral Bogan: As I remember, it was between the seventh and 12th of January 1945.

Q: So it was after the action around the Philippines and Luzon when you were hit on the 25th of November, and before . . .

Admiral Bogan: Before we went into the China Sea, we gave long-range support to MacArthur's landings in Lingayen Gulf in the early part of January, off the northern end of Luzon, and then went around the northern tip of the island and into the China Sea.

Q: And that was when you hit those islands?

Admiral Bogan: Yes, the Nansei Shoto Islands. But the first strikes were in the vicinity of Saigon and Camranh Bay, and then as we came out, we stopped and hit the islands and two days' bombardment of Hong Kong, and then back to another strike on

Formosa.

Q: But you did tremendous damage to Japanese shipping.

Admiral Bogan: In the China Sea, yes. We got several convoys, we sank two cruisers, I know, and we sank a French cruiser, La Motte-Piquet, which had been taken over by the Japs at Saigon. I think I covered that yesterday.

Q: You mentioned it, but I was trying in my own mind to get a clearer picture of the sequence of events. Wasn't that the time that Halsey made the comment that the Japs claimed a tremendous victory and then Halsey made his comment that . . .

Admiral Bogan: No. That was the previous October, about Formosa, when the Houston had been torpedoed and an antiaircraft cruiser was, which Ray Alexander had, was either torpedoed or mined. Anyway, she got back.

Q: Oh, I see. So the first visit was in October of '44 and the second one was in January '45.

Admiral Bogan: The second what?

Q: The second strike on Formosa and into the China Sea.

Bogan #2 - 145

Admiral Bogan: Well, we had two strikes on Formosa in October of '44, and then we hit it again in January '45, as we came out of the China Sea. And after that I believe they went up to Okinawa and hit it again and then back to Ulithi, and that's when I went on leave.

Q: Actually, by that time, as you say, Okinawa was actually the last gasp, wasn't it?

Admiral Bogan: Yes, that was 84 days from April til the first part of June.

Admiral Bogan: But from then on, the damage you had done both in the Philippines and in the China Sea and Indochina had wrecked their Navy.

Admiral Bogan: Wrecked their supply system and the ships that were at Kure. No, they never got out of there. They were anchored and we spent two days going over them.

Q: In the shipyard?

Admiral Bogan: No, it's a bay, a naval base there at Kure.

Q: Do you think we ever really needed to use that atomic bomb?

Admiral Bogan: As a necessity, I don't believe so, but to add the final push to a toppling empire and make them so they were ready to quit, that did. Those two bombs at Hiroshima and Nagasaki did it.

Q: I wondered what your thinking was on the wisdom of using them.

Admiral Bogan: I have doubts, but I mean the responsibility was not mine; the authority was not mine. I could just have an opinion, but it's not worth anything.

Q: Oh, sure it is.

Admiral Bogan: Well, I mean, it's my own. You can say things but when you're not responsible, as I'm not in this case, which I might not be able to do had I made the decision to drop the bomb, which Truman did.

Q: True. And always one can criticize after the fact, anyway, whereas perhaps in the same situation I would have said to do it. You can't tell. So, anyway, you did come back to Pearl. Where were you at the time the Japs surrendered?

Admiral Bogan: The last four days before the surrender, I was ordered to provide protective patrols for the troops which MacArthur was flying from the Philippines to Japan, and I split the task group into two sections, one under Admiral Clifton Sprague and the other I maintained myself, and we conducted a great many flight operations, dropping food on prisoner of war camps, and patrolling this area in which the planes were coming up from the Philippines with MacArthur's troops.* When the actual surrendered occurred, my group was about 200 miles southwest of Tokyo. The other three groups were to the east of Tokyo, and their planes east of and in the vicinity of Tokyo, their planes staged a great big flyover immediately following the surrender.

The following day we were on our way into Tokyo Bay and at a distance of about 20 miles we got radio orders to return immediately to Pearl Harbor--the Randolph did. I had the Indefatigable, a British carrier, in my group, and she went on in and I took two destroyers and went back to Pearl.

Q: Why didn't they let you go in?

Admiral Bogan: Oh, they wanted these ships to go back to start the Magic Carpet thing and bring the boys home to Mama.

---
*Rear Admiral Clifton A.F. Sprague, USN.

Q: It seems a shame that you weren't there for the . . .

Admiral Bogan: I had no curiosity.

Q: Didn't you?

Admiral Bogan: No. I've got a picture of all these guys on the Missouri, but I had no curiosity at all.

Q: So you didn't mind not being there, seeing the surrender ceremony?

Admiral Bogan: As a matter of fact, Admiral Sherman, whom I had relieved, was at that time in a cruiser and he was to take over. They were going to have task forces reorganized after the surrender.

Admiral Sherman was then in a cruiser, and he wanted that cruiser to proceed in to Tokyo to be present at the surrender. I told him that I wouldn't let the cruiser go, but I would see that he could fly in the next morning. He said, "The weather prediction is bad."

I said, "Maybe by your meteorologist, but it's all right from mine." So the next morning he flew from a carrier in to Tokyo and was present at the surrender.

After Pearl Harbor, our arrival at Pearl Harbor in the

Randolph, I was detached and flew back to San Diego.

Q: Before we leave the Pacific, though, I do want to mention again that you received the gold star in lieu of a second Distinguished Service Medal as Commander of Task Group 38.3, from July to September 1945. May I read it?

Admiral Bogan: If you wish.

Q: I'd like to, because I don't think you speak as well of yourself as you should.

"Rear Admiral Bogan pressed on a devastating attack on the home land of Japan in coordination with other task groups, directing destructive strikes against aircraft and supporting industries, installations, and transportation facilities and concentrations of naval vessels at Yokosuka, Kure, and Kobe. Under repeated aerial attacks delivered by the desperate Japanese, he maintained a high standard of fighting efficiency in all his gallant ships and employed brilliant defensive tactics in repulsing the fanatic enemy. His fearless leadership and expert tactical control of the carriers, battleships, cruisers, and destroyers in Task Group 38.3 were vital factors in the infliction of extensive damage on the enemy and in the completion of hazardous missions without damage to his own ship."

Admiral Bogan: I received the Gold Star for the period noted in that citation, but it was not presented to me until the following February at Norfolk, when I was ComAirLant, and Admiral Mitscher, who was at that time Commander Eighth Fleet, made the presentation.

Upon arrival at San Diego, I called Admiral Mitscher, who was in Washington, to inquire about my next orders, and he was fretting under conditions in the Navy Department at that time. So he told me over the telephone to take 30 days' leave and be happy "as you'll never be happy again." Following his advice, Katie and I went to . . .

Q: What did he mean?

Admiral Bogan: Well, just the letdown after the war.

Q: I was going to ask you how you felt at this time.

Admiral Bogan: So Katie and I--my wife--went to New York, and we had two very pleasant weeks there, and another week on the return with friends in Denver, and then proceeded to Naval Air Station Alameda, where I'd been ordered as Fleet Air Alameda. There was really no excuse for the job at that time. All activities had ceased. There was still a staff of better than 70 officers and men and women, hanging around headquarters trying to look busy and not succeeding. So in December I got a telephone call from Washington saying I could become the Commander Naval Air Force Atlantic Fleet, if I wished to, which meant an automatic promotion to vice admiral. I gladly took it, and I relieved Admiral Bellinger on the first of February 1946.* I spent the next three years, less one month, in that job, which was difficult because of the wholesale discharges which had followed the end of the war, and the arrival on two-year enlistments of a bunch of bright, selfish young men who wanted to avail themselves of a GI Bill of Rights, but had no loyalty to the Navy and merely did their two years so they could qualify for those benefits.**

We were short of men, we were short of talent, we were short of ships. We were short of everything, and it was a constant attempt to make do with what was available.

Q: How many ships were in the Atlantic Fleet then?

Admiral Bogan: Oh, there were a great many. The Sixth Fleet had been started. It was first called the Eighth Fleet and then the Sixth Fleet in the Mediterranean. And they were decommissioning ships as fast as they could do so, and put the crews on other ships which our commitments made us keep in commission. As a

---
*Vice Admiral Patrick N.L. Bellinger, USN.
**The GI Bill provided educational benefits and other benefits to former servicemen following World War II.

result, I would say that all ships had about three-fourths of their assigned complement and struggled very hard to carry out their duties in an efficient manner.

Q: What was the geographical area of the Atlantic Fleet?

Admiral Bogan: They didn't have a South Atlantic Fleet at that time, but the whole Atlantic Ocean.

Q: How far east did it go?

Admiral Bogan: As far as the coast of Europe.

Q: Clear to the coast?

Admiral Bogan: Yes.

Q: I thought that the command over there was the Sixth Fleet and then there was another command that went from England down around the coast of Europe.

Admiral Bogan: If there was, I don't remember it. Although the boundary used to be sort of accepted as $26°$ west longitude, and for ships in that area, that was our operating area. As far east as that. But the Sixth Fleet, you see, was not part of the

Atlantic Fleet.

Q: What were the commitments of the Air Force Atlantic in those days?

Admiral Bogan: It was really an administrative command, as Commander Air Force Pacific Fleet is now, for training all aircraft and ships that operate aircraft in the Atlantic Fleet and to meet the schedule put out by the Commander in Chief Atlantic or the Chief of Naval Operations.

Q: It's kind of hard to think back what was going on at the end of the war, because so many times one stops thinking with the surrender of Japan.

Admiral Bogan: Well, there was very little going on, and yet we had already begun this police action, but it turned out later that assistance to Greece, although the Navy, except as logistics was applied, was not very much concerned with that. And the Sixth Fleet in the Mediterranean, which had previously been the Eighth Fleet, was to keep a deterrent effect on the Russians moving into the Mediterranean, which they have now done.

Q: Sure. And you had that job for almost three years.

Bogan #2 - 154

Admiral Bogan: Three years less a month.

Q: I think it was during that period that Admiral Van Deurs tells of your coming aboard the Philippine Sea for underway training.*

Admiral Bogan: On occasion. It happened about every three months. Certain members of my staff and myself would fly to Guantanamo, and in conjunction with the fleet training personnel based there permanently, to conduct an operational readiness inspection of the ship, which had completed, in the case of a new ship, its shakedown, and in the case of a ship which had been overhauled, its training before joining the fleet again.

Q: Van Deurs's comment was that he took the Philippine Sea out of the Brooklyn Navy Yard in the fall of '47 and had some underway training. He had green officers and green crew and a new air group, and he had qualified them when you came in to Guantanamo for an inspection. This was when you had told him you didn't care for any honors, and he gave them to you anyway, and you made it very emphatic when you said you didn't want honors you meant you didn't want honors.

---

*Rear Admiral George Van Deurs, USN, whose oral history is in the Naval Institute collection.

Admiral Bogan: Probably so.

Q: But I'm sure it was just an incident in a day's work to you.

Admiral Bogan: That's right. It was.

Q: Anyway, you impressed him very much.

Admiral Bogan: I'd known George since we were young people. We'd never been on the same squadron, nor do I remember being in the same duty with him, but I've known him casually for a good many years.

Q: Well, he's a great admirer of you.

Admiral Bogan: That's fine.
Then on the first of January '49, I took command of the First Fleet at San Diego. The First Fleet then and now is really the training organization of the Pacific Fleet, which prepares new ships, newly overhauled ships, readiness to join the fleet, in the Seventh Fleet, for instance, in the Western Pacific. And shortly after taking over, we made a cruise to Alaska in the latter part of January for cold weather landing experience with a group of Marines. It just happened that in a change in the weather of that area around Kodiak, when we got there it was not

only cold, but it was clear and very little wind. So it was more or less a lark for the Marines, and no difficulty to be found. We returned then to San Diego and operated with North Island as a base, or the <u>Albemarle</u> or another tender as a flagship, until the following November when we conducted the Miki operation.

Q: I don't know that.

Admiral Bogan: Which was the landing of two divisions of troops from Fort Lewis, Washington, on the beaches at Honolulu. It went off pretty well, but that was my last active command, and I retired the following February first.

Q: I wanted, before we go on, to talk a little bit about the experiences you had, not necessarily with command, but with the Secretary of the Navy. Wasn't this a period during which--now I'm quoting Jocko Clark--that Captain Crommelin released a confidential letter that you had written to Secretary Matthews deploring the low morale in the Navy due to lack of funds and the unsympathetic attitude in the Defense Department, and he gave as his reason that he wanted a congressional inquiry?[*] Is that an accurate . . ?

---

[*]Captain John G. Crommelin, Jr., USN; Secretary of the Navy Francis P. Matthews.

Admiral Bogan: Well, it's true to a certain extent. Secretary Matthews--fortunately, now dead--was a lawyer from Omaha who had amassed a tremendous fortune by handling grazing rights on federal lands in the West. He professed ardent Catholicism and had a chapel in his home in Omaha, and I think he was a man of very small stature. At any rate, in October of '49, he invited all flag officers to write to him expressing their opinion of the existing morale in the Navy and the causes for it. He invited this letter, and I wrote it and forwarded it through channels, Commander in Chief Pacific Fleet, which was Radford, and he forwarded it with this endorsement: "Admiral Bogan is an officer of great ability and wide experience of naval aviation. No question of his sincerity and high principles. I know that the writing of this letter was motivated by sincere patriotism. Rightly or wrongly, the majority of officers of the Pacific Fleet concurred with Captain Crommelin and with the ideas expressed by Vice Admiral Bogan, but most of them avoid any statements to that effect, but they would probably question the timing of such public statement. Nevertheless, it would be a great mistake to underestimate the depth and sincerity of their feelings. Because of my conviction that this letter is representative of the general feeling, I commend it to your attention."

Now, Raddy sent that to the Secretary. There's the letter. In September '49, Secretary Matthews sent a letter to all flag officers inviting their comment on the state of morale in the

Navy. According to that invitation, I wrote this letter to him. Do you want me to read it?

Q: But why is the subject "Comment on a statement of Captain Crommelin"?

Admiral Bogan: Because Captain Crommelin was sounding off all over the country. He was up at Alameda at the time. He's almost a psychopathic case.

Q: Oh, yes.

Admiral Bogan: And creating a great deal of publicity. He was also in this OP-23 in the Navy Department at the time. So when I wrote this original letter, and I forwarded a copy to him in the Navy Department, and without my concurrence or even telling me about it, he arranged a secret meeting with the press in the elevator of the Press Club in Washington and handed them this letter. It created a great deal of publicity all over the country. I've got in that file several comments from the press. Now the Secretary's aide at that time told me later that my letter had been on his desk for five days and he hadn't read it and hadn't done anything about it, but, he said, when Crommelin gave it to the press and it was published all over, the muck really hit the fan. Those were his exact words.

Bogan #2 - 159

Q: I can imagine so.

Admiral Bogan: Now you can see here. Here's an acknowledgement on the eighth of October from Matthews: "Dear Admiral Bogan, your communication of 20 September has been forwarded to me by the Office of the Chief of Naval Operations. As soon as time permits, I shall write you further with respect to this document and your procedure in handling it." See, he's got this listed "Secret and Personal." There was nothing irregular in my handling of the thing.

Q: And I will attach it if I may.

Admiral Bogan: You surely may. Now, the aftermath of that was that I was in Pearl Harbor on this Miki operation when I got this thing. When I got back here, I had some inkling that I was going to be sent to Jacksonville as fleet air in a job subordinate to the one that I'd had for three years, and I made my plans to retire if necessary.

Q: This was obviously Matthews's point.

Admiral Bogan: Well, wait til I come to the end of it.

Q: Excuse me.

Admiral Bogan: So then I got a letter from John Price, who was a classmate of mine and was Vice Chief of Naval Operations, and he said there'd be no decision about Jacksonville until he came out here on a certain date.* Three days before that date, I found my orders to Jacksonville, which meant going back to rear admiral after four years, so I put in a request for retirement, and I said if it weren't for public press that I'm being demoted, I hereby request retirement from the First Fleet on February first. Then Crommelin . . .

Q: You heard about that by reading about it?

Admiral Bogan: In the public press, about the orders to Jacksonville. Then Crommelin again sent this so-called newspaper reporter down from San Francisco to interview me one night. He got himself very drunk, and when I had to go across the street for some purpose, he telephoned the San Diego newspapers and he telephoned the Los Angeles newspapers from this house setting me up for a press conference with them the next day.

Q: Unknown to you?

Admiral Bogan: Unknown to me. Next morning the telephone rang,

---
*Admiral John Dale Price, USN.

"What have you got to say at this press conference, Admiral?"

I said, "I don't know anything about a press conference."

He said, "We got a call from your agent last night saying there would be a press conference."

Q: Who was calling you?

Admiral Bogan: The local press and the Los Angeles press. I said, "There's no press conference. I'm going to attend a Republican Women's Club luncheon today, but I have no press conference scheduled or intended." But when I got down there, there were two reporters from the San Diego papers, and they asked me if I'd give them a little background on this letter. I told them that the letter had been widely published and that Secretary Matthews had said that any letters he received in reply to his invitation would receive serious consideration. I said, "In my case, the only consideration I'm positive I received had him refer to me in very derogatory terms to a committee of the Congress and also questioning the handling of my letter." Well, that was fine.

Q: What did he say to Congress?

Admiral Bogan: Well, he said—it was at the time of that investigation, you know, the B-36 and all the rest, and I've forgotten what he said. I had the Congressional Record at one time, but I don't have it now.

Q: But he spoke in derogatory terms about you?

Admiral Bogan: About me, and I think it was mostly about the handling of this letter without justification, because I was within my rights. So the next day I went flying, and when I came back from flying, here was Tommy Sprague at North Island to meet me, and he said, "I have orders to relieve you immediately."* This was a week before I was due to retire. I was ordered to temporary duty in the 11th Naval District, went back to rear admiral for a week, so I would not retire with four stars with a gun deck promotion on retirement at that time, and that was it. And Forrest Sherman and Matthews did that together.** Sprague said that he argued with Forrest Sherman about it, but Sherman said, "The decision's been taken. Shut up."

Q: Forrest Sherman was Nimitz's chief of staff, wasn't he?

Admiral Bogan: Yes, but at that time he was Chief of Naval Operations. He had been Chief of Naval Operations only about

---
*Vice Admiral Thomas L. Sprague, USN.
**Admiral Forrest P. Sherman, USN, Chief of Naval Operations from 1949 to 1951.

three weeks, after Denfeld was kicked out, again on all this stuff, and he became Chief of Naval Operations.* He was Vice Chief of Naval Operations when Nimitz was Chief, just after the war.

Q: Do you think that Sherman had a lot of influence on Nimitz?

Admiral Bogan: Oh, he had a great deal of influence. But that has nothing to do with me.

Q: I want to ask you about a few other perhaps personal things, although I guess the time of your retirement officially closes your naval career.

Admiral Bogan: It did.

Q: Tell me what you've done and what your interests have been since then.

Admiral Bogan: Shortly following retirement, I signed a contract with a life insurance company in Dallas, Texas, which was rewarding financially, but a great embarrassment to me, because I found out that they were a very unscrupulous group of people. At

---

*Admiral Louis M. Denfeld, USN, Chief of Naval Operations from 1947 to 1949.

the termination of the contract, I brought suit for money which they had illegally withheld from my contract, and the judge directed the jury to find for me if the company did not compromise. When the jury found out that my attorney and the company's attorney had reached a compromise on 80% of the amount requested, the jury, as a group, came by me and told me that I was foolish to have agreed to that compromise because they were going to award me three times what I was asking. But my counsel told me, "If you take this reward now that they'll undoubtedly give you, they'll merely appeal and it will be three years before the case comes up again." I wanted to be clear, and I was.

Q: The money probably wasn't the important thing to you anyway, was it?

Admiral Bogan: Well, not the most. No. I had no other commercial interests for a long time, but a few years ago I did take a 12-month contract with the Kamam Helicopter Company, which the president of the company told me was very much to their advantage. I suggested at the end of the year that the contract not be renewed, because people with whom I had worked in the Navy Department were no longer there, and I did not want to go in and try to be a door-opener. That about concludes the commercial interests. At home, I try to keep in shape. I try to keep abreast of current events, do a great deal of reading, I think, and try to live peacefully with my fellow man.

Q: I like very much the poem you gave me, which you said you do, in fact, live by, and I'm going to attach that to the biography, if I may.

Admiral Bogan: Most certainly so.

Q: And I want to read from a book, the title of which is Flattop, and it is a story of carriers by Barrett Gallagher, which I think is a tribute to you, and I'm sure it's factual.* The title of it is "Strong Opinion and Outspoken Eloquence," and it shows your picture and goes on to say you were a fighter both in the ring and at sea.

"He had been on jeep carriers in the Marianas before moving up to the big ships. Known equally for his strong opinions and his outspoken eloquence, he usually spoke in a misleading soft voice that masked a furious impatience for any pretense or incompetence. Bogan was a hard man to work for, but he was also one of those tough operators who commanded respect and loyalty from his staff and from everyone under him because he measured up to his own standards. The term 'he's a Bogan man' became a

---

*Barrett Gallagher, Flattop (Garden City, New York: Doubleday, 1959). Gallagher was one of the photographers who covered the Pacific war as part of Commander Edward Steichen's team.

password in many circles. To satisfy Bogan, a man had to be good at his job."

And, you know what, I would have liked working for you very much.

Admiral Bogan: I don't think I was. I could tell you sometime, some seaman was very mad. I was a younger officer and I'd done something, I've forgotten what, and he said, "I'll tell you this, commander, you're a real son of a bitch, but you're square."

Q: Well, that is the kind of--I understand that. I hate incompetence, and unfortunately there's a lot of it today.

Admiral Bogan: Incompetence in the atmosphere and under the conditions in which we were operating. You just couldn't take it. You had to get good men.

Q: Of course. Well, should we bring this to a close now?

Admiral Bogan: Well, unless you want that King thing.

Q: I would like you to tell that to me.

Admiral Bogan: My last meeting with Admiral King occurred in the Navy Department in the late fall of 1946, I believe. He had just returned from Oxford, where he had been given an honorary degree of some kind, and his enthusiasm and admiration for Clementine Churchill, Winston's wife, was greater than I'd ever heard him express for a human being before. After and during the course of our conversation, he suggested that I see something which he had received while he was in England, and went to the transom on the side of this combination office-living quarters that he used in the Navy Department, and brought back a little morocco-bound folder. He started to hand it to me, and then said, "No. I don't think I will." I told him that I hadn't asked to see it. It was his offer, so he said, "Oh, go ahead and read it." It was a very laudatory message on parchment, thanking him for his assistance to the British during the war in the way of aircraft and ships, and it was signed by the top British military people and Winston Churchill. Having had some experience on Admiral King's staff during the war, during the time referred to, I realized that it was a rather belated acknowledgement of assistance which had been given to the best extent that he could, but never measured up to the exorbitant demands which were made on him by the British. I started to hand it back with the remark, "Well, this is too little, too late," and I looked up and, much to my surprise, tears were running down his cheeks. So I quickly turned away and took the folder back to the transom, while he wiped his eyes, and after a few more words, he said, "Jerry, do you think I've changed much with the years?"

I replied, "Admiral, you may have mellowed a little bit, but I would still hate to get you mad."

The last words he ever said to me were, with a smile, "Get out of my office, you son of a bitch."

Q: That was affection from him, perhaps?

Admiral Bogan: It was friendly.

Q: Well, I've enjoyed this. Do you have any other comments that you'd like to make?

Admiral Bogan: No, I think I'm dry.

Q: I hope it hasn't been tiring.

Admiral Bogan: Oh, it hasn't, not a bit, no.

Q: I do thank you for my sake and for the Institute.

Admiral Bogan: I hope it makes sense when it's in one piece.

THE MAN IN THE GLASS

When you get what you want in your struggle for self
And the world makes you king for a day,
Just go to a mirror and look at yourself,
And see what THAT man has to say.

For it isn't your father or mother or wife
Whose judgment upon you must pass;
The Fellow whose verdict counts most in your life
Is the one staring back from the glass.

You may be like Jack Horner and chisel a plum
And think you're a wonderful guy,
But the man in the glass says you're only a bum
If you can't look him straight in the eye.

He's the fellow to please, never mind all the rest,
For he's with you clear up to the end,
And you've passed your most dangerous, difficult test
If the man in the glass is your friend.

You may fool the whole world down the pathway of years
And get pats on the back as you pass,
But your final reward will be heartaches and tears
If you've cheated the man in the glass.

Index

to

Reminiscences of

Vice Admiral Gerald F. Bogan

U.S. Navy (Retired)

U.S. Naval Institute

Annapolis, Maryland

1986

Aging
  Bogan's attitude toward, pages 15-16

Air Force Atlantic Fleet
  Commitments in mid-1940s, page 153

Aircraft - Experimental
  Tested by Navy pilots at Anacostia in the early 1930s, pages 51-53

Aircraft Battle Force
  Type command headed by Captain J.M. Reeves in the mid-1920s, pages 34, 38

Aircraft Carriers
  USS Langley (CV-1) operates on the West Coast in the late 1920s with J.M. Reeves embarked as Commander Aircraft Battle Force, pages 31, 34-38; USS Langley change of fighter squadrons in the early 1930s, pages 40-41; USS Lexington (CV-2) a taut ship under Captain Ernest J. King, 1930-1932, pages 54-55; Lexington's air squadrons and operations in mid-1930s, pages 56, 58; Bogan's experience in making carrier landings, pages 47-48; Morrow Board of 1925 recommended that only naval aviators command carriers, page 57; USS Saratoga (CV-3) makes mock attack on Hawaii in 1932, pages 44-46; Saratoga compared with Lexington in the early 1930s, pages 54-55; Saratoga's operations in the South Pacific in 1942 and Bogan's injury on board, pages 78-84; USS Yorktown (CV-5) in fleet exercises in the Caribbean in the late 1930s, pages 64, 66-70; Yorktown in the Pacific in 1939, page 71; operations of the escort carriers of Carrier Division 25 around Hawaii and in support of Saipan in mid-1944, pages 93-104; USS Bonhomme Richard (CV-31) training off Leyte in June 1945, pages 141-142; USS Belleau Wood (CVL-24) attacked by kamikaze in October 1944, page 106; USS Essex (CV-9) as Bogan's flagship in mid-1944, page 104; USS Franklin (CV-13) attacked by kamikazes in October 1944, page 104; Franklin is terribly damaged by Japanese bombs in March 1945, pages 131-136; USS Hancock (CV-19) rescues Franklin survivors, pages 134, 138; USS Independence (CVL-22) operations at Leyte Gulf in October 1944, pages 109-110; Independence off Indochina in early 1945, page 130; USS Intrepid attacked by kamikazes in November 1944, pages 115-123, 128-129; USS Lexington (CV-16) as Bogan's flagship in late 1944, pages 118, 125-126; USS Randolph (CV-15) hit by both a Japanese kamikaze and U.S. Army plane in early 1945, pages 131, 137-138; Randolph part of Magic Carpet operation at war's end, pages 138, 147; USS Philippine Sea (CV-47) takes Bogan on training cruise in 1947, page 154

Alameda
  See Fleet Air Alameda

Anacostia, D.C.
  Site of Navy aircraft testing in the early 1930s, pages 51-53

Andrews, Vice Admiral Adolphus, USN (USNA, 1901)
  As Commandant Third Naval District and Commander Eastern Sea Frontier, criticized by Bogan for having ineffective ASW setup in 1943, page 87

Andrews, Rear Admiral Phillip, USN (USNA, 1886)
  Commander Naval Forces Eastern Mediterranean in 1919 popular with Italian kids, page 14

Antiaircraft Gunnery
  Battleships New Jersey (BB-62) and Iowa (BB-61) shoot down Japanese planes off the Philippines in November 1944, page 120

Antisubmarine Warfare (ASW)
  Birmingham (CL-2) made patrols off Atlantic coast during World War I, page 10; pilots at Naval Air Station Miami perform patrols in the Gulf of Mexico in the early 1940s, pages 74-75, 78; Tenth Fleet's ASW effort in 1943, pages 85-87

Army Air Corps, U.S.
  Participates in mock attack on Oahu in February 1932, page 45

Army Air Forces, U.S.
  P-38 causes great damage to Randolph (CV-15) in early 1945, pages 137-138

Aroostock, USS (CM-3)
  Rescues Bogan after an unsuccessful carrier landing on Langley (CV-1) in the mid-1920s, pages 35-36

Atlantic Fleet
  Scope of responsibility after World War II, page 152

Atomic Bomb
  Bogan's thoughts on use of atomic bombs to end World War II, page 146

Auckland, New Zealand
  Bogan recuperates from fall off Saratoga (CV-3) flight deck in 1943, pages 82-84

Aviation Cadet Program
  Individuals trained at Pensacola in the late 1930s proved to be excellent officers after reaching the fleet, pages 58-61

Aviation Training
  Quality of instruction at Pensacola in the early 1920s, pages 30-31; Navy's policy on age, pages 31-32; Bogan's fellow students in the mid-1920s, page 32; more senior officers trained at Pensacola in the 1920s and 1930s to provide leadership for air commands, pages 38-39; steps for flunking or keeping students, page 40; naval aviation cadet program in late 1930s produced excellent officers, pages 58-61; carrier training done at Naval Air Station Miami while Corpus Christi under construction in the early 1940s, pages 71-72

Aviators
   Balance needed between enthusiasm and discipline, pages 45-46; Bogan's view that the planes of the 1960s required sharper pilot skills than those he flew, pages 46-47; individuals unsuited to aviation, pages 47-48

Bahamas
   Naval Air Station Miami offers ASW patrols to the governor of the Bahamas in the early 1940s, but is declined, page 75

Baker, Rear Admiral Wilder D., USN   (USNA, 1914)
   Admiral McCain's chief of staff, Baker, argues with Bogan about disposition of Intrepid (CV-11) planes after the ship is attacked in late 1944, page 117

Belleau Wood, USS (CVL-24)
   Attacked by kamikaze during October 1944 Formosa raid, page 106

Bidwell, Lieutenant Commander Abel T., USN   (USNA, 1908)
   Bogan contacts former shipmate Bidwell in Bureau of Navigation in 1919 for a destroyer assignment, page 17

Birmingham, USS (CL-2)
   ASW patrols off Atlantic coast during World War I, page 10; convoy duty, pages 10-11; anecdote about whale mistaken for enemy sub, page 12; gun battery, page 12

Blacks
   Rear Admiral A.C. Read reportedly relieved of duty in Chicago in 1944 after suggesting no more blacks be sent there, page 89

Blakely, Rear Admiral Charles A., USN   (USNA, 1903)
   Commandant of Naval Air Station Pensacola approached about Captain John McCain's progress as a student pilot in the mid-1930s, pages 61-62

Blood, Lieutenant Commander Russell H., MC, USNR
   Treats Bogan for head injury at Auckland in 1943, page 83

Boeing Corporation
   Fighting planes tested by Navy pilots at Anacostia in the early 1930s, page 51

Bogan, Vice Admiral Gerald F., USN   (USNA, 1916)
   Decorations, pages 98, 119, 123-124, 149-150; health, pages 81-85, 88, 136-137; wife, pages 83, 150; parents, pages 1-2; Naval Academy midshipman from 1912-1916, pages 2-8; teaches third grade to recruits at Great Lakes, 1916-1917, pages 8-10; division and gunnery officer in Birmingham (CL-2) during World War I, pages 10-13; duty in Stribling (DD-96), 1919, pages 13-16; chief engineer, Hopewell (DD-181), 1919-1920, pages 17-18; executive officer, USS Broome (DD-210), 1920-1921, pages 18, 25-27; commanding officer, naval radio station, Russian Island, 1922, pages 18-24; instructor at USNA, 1923-1924, pages 5-6, 28; flight school, Pensacola, 1924-1925, pages 29-33; executive

officer and commanding officer, Fighting Squadron One, 1925-1928, pages 34-40; Commander Squadron One and Wing Commander of Landplanes, Pensacola, 1928-1930, pages 32-33, 40; Commander Fighting Squadron Three, 1930-1931, pages 40-43, 90-92; Commander Fighting Squadron One, 1931-1932, pages 41, 44-45, 50; flight test officer, Anacostia, 1932-1934, pages 50-53; air officer, USS Lexington (CV-2), 1934-1936, pages 53-58; superintendent of aviation training, Pensacola, 1936-1937, pages 58-62; executive officer, Pensacola naval air station, 1937-1938, page 63; navigator, USS Yorktown (CV-5), 1938-1939, pages 63-70; executive officer, USS Yorktown (CV-5), 1939-1940, pages 64-65, 71; commanding officer, Naval Air Station Miami, 1940-1942, pages 71-78; commanding officer, USS Saratoga (CV-3), 1942-1943, pages 78-84; Commander Naval Air, Tenth Fleet, 1943, pages 85-87; Commander Fleet Air, Norfolk, 1943-1944, pages 88-90, 92; Commander Carrier Division 25, 1944, pages 93-104; Commander Carrier Division Four and Commander Task Group 58.4, 1944, pages 104-141; Commander Task Group 38.3, 1944-1945, pages 141-149; Commander Fleet Air Alameda, 1945-1946, pages 150-151; Commander Naval Air Force Atlantic Fleet, 1945-1948, pages 151-155; Commander First Fleet, 1949-1950, pages 155-156, 159, 162; circumstances precipitating Bogan's retirement on 1 February 1950, pages 156-163; post-retirement activities, pages 163-165

Bolger, Captain Joseph F., USN (USNA, 1921A)
Intrepid (CV-11) commanding officer orders ship to heel during kamikaze attack in November 1944 to rid excess gas and water, page 122

Bolsheviks
Demand Russian Island radio station from U.S. Navy in 1922, pages 20-22; in Polish-Russian war, pages 25-26

Bonhomme Richard, USS (CV-31)
Trains off Leyte in June 1945 for Okinawa campaign, pages 141-142

Britain
See England; Royal Navy

Broome, USS (DD-210)
Mediterranean cruise in mid-1920, page 18; ordered with division to the Philippines in January 1921, page 18; in Riga at conclusion of Polish-Russian War in 1920, pages 25-27

Brown, Captain Charles R., USN (USNA, 1921B)
Commands Kalinin Bay (CVE-68) during mid-1944 Saipan action, page 96

"Brownshoes" Versus "Blackshoes"
Rivalry between non-aviators and pilots, pages 49-50

Burke, Commodore Arleigh A., USN (USNA, 1923)
As Vice Admiral Marc Mitscher's chief of staff at Leyte Gulf in October 1944, pages 109, 141

Cagle, Rear Admiral Malcolm W., USN (USNA, 1941)
   Bogan's former flag secretary takes him out in the Enterprise (CVAN-65) in the late 1960s, page 46

Carrier Aviation
   See Aircraft Carriers

Carrier Division 25
   Patrols from Pearl Harbor in 1944, page 93; makeup of division, pages 93-94; operations in support of the Saipan campaign in June-July 1944, pages 94-104;

Chance-Vought
   Bombers tested by Navy pilots at Anacostia in the early 1930s, page 51

China Sea
   Action by Task Force 38 in 1945, pages 143-145

Churchill, Clementine
   Fleet Admiral King highly impressed by Winston Churchill's wife after visit in 1946, page 167

Churchill, Sir Winston
   Presents Fleet Admiral Ernest King with a citation in 1946 in belated thanks for wartime service, page 167

Cold Weather Training
   Warm front passes through during an Alaskan training exercise for Marines in 1949, pages 155-156

Communications
   U.S. Navy radio station on Russian Island turned over to the Soviets in 1922, pages 19-22

Communism
   Bogan's experience with Communism in Russian Island in the early 1920s, pages 22-24

Convoys
   Escorted to France by the USS Birmingham during World War I, pages 10-11

Crommelin, Captain John G., Jr., USN (USNA, 1923)
   Releases to the press a letter concerning Navy morale that Bogan wrote to SecNav Francis Matthews in September 1949, pages 156-162

Damage Control
   Control of flooding in the escort carrier Fanshaw Bay (CVE-70) after she was hit by a Japanese bomb off Saipan in June 1944, pages 101-102; fire fighting in the carrier Franklin (CV-13) after she was hit by Japanese bombs in March 1945, pages 133-135

Davison, Rear Admiral Ralph E., USN (USNA, 1916)
    Commanded Task Force 38.4 during October 1944 Formosa raid, page 106; in Leyte Gulf action, October 1944, pages 108, 114

Demobilization
    Rapid loss of personnel causes great difficulties for Bogan as Commander Naval Air Force Atlantic Fleet in the late 1940s, pages 151-152

Douglas Aircraft
    Bombers tested by Navy pilots at Anacostia in the early 1930s, page 51

Duke of Windsor
    Had little power as governor of the Bahamas in World War II, page 75

Education
    Benefits to career from Naval Academy training, page 5; Ensign Bogan teaches third grade to recruits at Great Lakes, Illinois, in 1916, pages 8-10

Edward VIII
    As governor of the Bahamas in the early 1940s, the former British King is offered ASW patrols by Naval Air Station Miami, but declines, page 75

Eighth Fleet
    Becomes the Sixth Fleet in late 1940s, pages 151, 153

England
    Deteriorated quality of young men to choose from for military service at the outset of World War II, pages 72-73

Escort Carriers
    See Carrier Division 25

Essex, USS (CV-9)
    Bogan's flagship during Guam air support operation in 1944, page 104

Evans, Lynden (Democrat-Illinois)
    Congressman from Chicago appoints Bogan to U.S. Naval Academy in 1912, pages 2-3

Ewen, Captain Edward, USN (USNA, 1921)
    Talked with Bogan about Japanese ships in San Bernardino Strait in October 1944, page 109; Bogan felt message Independence (CVL-22) skipper Ewen sent to Halsey regarding Leyte Gulf action was not strong enough to attract attention, pages 113-114

Experimental Aircraft
    Tested by Navy pilots at Anacostia in the early 1930s, pages 51-53

Fanshaw Bay, USS (CVE-70)
  At Saipan in 1944, pages 94, 96-97; attacked by a Japanese plane on 17 June 1944, pages 101-102; receives Presidential Unit Citation, page 103

Far Eastern Republic
  U.S. signs agreement with this Russian province to set up radio station in the early 1920s, pages 18-20

Fear
  Reactions among those in ships attacked by kamikazes in World War II, pages 135-137

Fighting Squadron One (VF-1)
  Bogan loses a plane in the mid-1920s during Commander Aircraft Battle Force Captain "Bull" Reeves's effort to break the single day carrier landing record under conditions that showed the commander didn't understand aviation, pages 34-37; pilots put in a perilous position by Reeves in the mid-1920s to impress Secretary of the Navy Curtis Wilbur, pages 37-38; part of war game that attacks Oahu in February 1932, page 44

Fighting Squadron Three (VF-3)
  Replaces enlisted squadron (VF-2) on Langley (CV-1) in the early 1930s, page 41; awards won under Bogan's leadership, page 42; seven of 18 officers made flag rank, pages 42-43

Fighting Squadron Two (VF-2)
  Bogan's VF-3 replaces this enlisted squadron on Langley (CV-1) in the early 1930s, pages 40-41

First Fleet, U.S.
  As training organization for Pacific Fleet in the late 1940s, pages 155-156

Fleet Air Alameda
  Superfluous command Bogan held from October 1945 to February 1946, page 150

Flight Pay
  Argument between blackshoes and brownshoes about fairness, pages 49-50

Formosa
  Bombed by Task Force 38 in October 1944, pages 106, 145; attacked by Task Group 38.2 in January 1945, pages 144-145

Franklin, USS (CV-13)
  Attacked by kamikazes during October 1944 Formosa raid, page 106; becomes Bogan's flagship when Randolph (CV-15) attacked in March 1945, page 131; hit by bombs on 19 March 1945, pages 131-134; crew's reaction to attack, pages 135-136

GI Bill
  Bogan felt the benefits offered to veterans at the end of World War II created problems such as rapid demobilization, page 151

Greece
U.S. involvement with Greece in the late 1940s, page 153

Grumman Corporation
Fighter-scout planes tested by Navy pilots at Anacostia in the early 1930s, page 51

Guadalcanal
Saratoga (CV-3) patrols off Guadalcanal in late 1942, pages 79-80

Guam
Japanese planes that attacked at Saipan in 1944 came from Guam, page 99; Task Force 58 provides air support in 1944, pages 104-105

Halsey, Admiral William F., Jr., USN (USNA, 1904)
Assessed as commandant of the Pensacola naval air station in the mid-1930s, page 63; angered by indecisive Yorktown (CV-5) commanding officer in the late 1930s, pages 66-67; anecdote from Bogan's convalescence in Solace (AH-5) reaches Halsey, page 82; at Leyte Gulf in October 1944, pages 107-114; sends ships into typhoon on 18 December 1944 despite warning from Bogan, pages 125-128

Hancock, USS (CV-19)
Picks up Franklin (CV-13) survivors in March 1945, pages 134, 138

Holt, Commander Harry E., USN
Served as enlisted pilot in VF-2 in the early 1930s, page 41

Hopewell, USS (DD-181)
Drastic measures to enlist crew after World War I, page 17; training cruise to Cuba in 1919, pages 17-18

Houston, USS (CL-81)
Attacked by torpedo in October 1944, pages 106, 144

Hull, USS (DD-350)
Lost in a typhoon in December 1944, pages 125-127

Independence, USS (CVL-22)
Operated night air group during Battle of Leyte Gulf in October 1944, pages 109-110; air group destroys Japanese planes at Saigon in early 1945, page 130

Indochina
Task Group 38.2 operates around Saigon in early 1945, pages 130, 143-144

Ingalls, David S.
As Assistant Secretary of the Navy for Aviation in the early 1920s, replaces enlisted fighter squadron in the USS Langley (CV-1), pages 40-41

Intrepid, USS (CV-11)
    Bogan's flagship attacked by kamikazes in November 1944, pages 115-123, 133; Halsey shows Bogan movie of Intrepid's attack at Christmas dinner in 1944, pages 121-122, 128-129

Iowa, USS (BB-61)
    Antiaircraft gunnery during Japanese air attack in November 1944, pages 120, 123

Italy
    American ship visits in 1919, page 14

Japan
    Interest in Russian Island in 1918, pages 18, 20; patrols from Kavieng in late 1942, page 81; propaganda reports about sinking U.S. carrier fleet in late 1944, pages 106-107; surrender in 1945, pages 147-148

Kalinin Bay, USS (CVE-68)
    At Saipan in 1944, pages 94, 96; sent to Eniwetok in mid-1944 for extra planes, page 100

Kaman Helicopter Company
    Bogan works for Kaman briefly after his Navy retirement, page 164

Kamikazes
    Attack on Fanshaw Bay (CVE-70) at Saipan in 1944, page 101; attacks on U.S. carriers during October 1944 Formosa raid, page 106; attack on Intrepid (CV-11) on 25 November 1944, pages 115-123; attack on Randolph (CV-15) in March 1945 forces Bogan to change flagships, page 131

Kavieng, New Ireland
    Japanese patrols in late 1942, page 81

Kidd, Lieutenant Isaac C., USN (USNA, 1906)
    Zealous officer at U.S. Naval Academy in the mid-1910s, later killed at Pearl Harbor, page 6

King, Fleet Admiral Ernest J., USN (USNA, 1901)
    Assessed as a pilot, page 39; credited with enforcing discipline as commanding officer of the Lexington (CV-2) in the early 1930s, pages 54-55; gives Bogan temporary assignment with Tenth Fleet in 1943 until he can regain his health, pages 85-86; breaks promise to Bogan to send him to sea in 1943, pages 87-90; gives Bogan excellent fitness reports despite disparaging oral comments, pages 90-91; attitude toward reprimands, pages 91-92; taken with Clementine Churchill during visit to Oxford in 1946, page 167; Bogan has a poignant final meeting with King in late fall of 1946, pages 166-168

Kinkaid, Vice Admiral Thomas C., USN (USNA, 1908)
    Question of responsibility at Leyte Gulf in October 1944, pages 111-112

Knox, Frank
  Secretary of the Navy Knox pressured by Eleanor Roosevelt to remove "Putty" Read from Chicago training billet after he made controversial racial statement in 1944, page 89

Kure
  Japanese naval base at Kure attacked in early 1945, pages 143, 145, 149

Kurita, Vice Admiral Takeo, IJN
  At Leyte Gulf in October 1944, pages 108, 112, 114

Langley, USS (CV-1)
  Operated from the West Coast in the mid-1920s, page 31; embarked Commander Aircraft Battle Force, Captain J.M. Reeves, shows lack of understanding of aviation by trying to break record for carrier landings in spite of adverse conditions, pages 34-38; enlisted squadron VF-2 replaced by Bogan's VF-3 in the early 1930s, pages 40-41

Leadership
  Bogan assessed by Flattop author Barrett Gallagher, pages 165-166

Lexington, USS (CV-2)
  Described as a taut ship under Captain Ernest J. King in the early 1930s, pages 54-55; squadrons embarked in the mid-1930s, page 56; air operations in the mid-1930s, page 58

Lexington, USS (CV-16)
  Bogan changes flagship to Lexington after Intrepid (CV-11) is attacked in November 1944, pages 118, 125; weathers typhoon in December 1944, page 126

Leyte Gulf, Battle of
  Bogan recounts October 1944 action from a carrier task group commander's perspective, pages 107-114

Loening, Grover
  Designed unsuccessful submarine-based plane in the early 1930s, pages 52-53

MacArthur, General Douglas, USA (USMA, 1903)
  Halsey speeds to support MacArthur in December 1944, risking his ships in a typhoon, page 125; Navy supports MacArthur's landing at Luzon, pages 129, 143; takes troops from Philippines to Japan just prior to Japanese signing of surrender, page 147

Matthews, Francis P.
  Secretary of the Navy in September 1949 solicits opinions from flag officers and then tries to demote Bogan when his suggestions are released to the press, pages 156-162

McCain, Vice Admiral John S., USN (USNA, 1906)
  Flight instructor questions his ability, but McCain receives

his wings in 1936 anyway, pages 61-62; at Leyte Gulf in October 1944, pages 108, 114; proposed handling of Intrepid (CV-11) planes after 1944 kamikaze attack, page 117; assessed by Bogan, pages 118-119

McWhorter, Rear Admiral Ernest D., USN (USNA, 1907)
Nervous Yorktown (CV-5) skipper in the late 1930s angers Halsey with indecisiveness, pages 65-68; promoted to flag rank but unsuccessful in first assignment, pages 66-67

Media
Publicize Bogan's private, solicited letter to Secretary of the Navy Matthews concerning Navy morale in 1949, pages 158, 160-161

Medicine
Treatment of Bogan by Navy doctors and nurses following injury in 1943, pages 82-85, 88-89

Mediterranean
Sixth Fleet patrols Mediterranean as deterrent to Russians in late 1940s, page 153

Miami, Florida, Naval Air Station
Carrier training done here in the early 1940s while Corpus Christi under construction, pages 71-72; description of facilities and program, pages 72-73, 76; called upon to perform antisubmarine patrols in the Gulf, pages 74-75, 78; mobilization after Japanese attack Pearl Harbor, page 77

Midway, USS (CVE-63)
At Saipan in 1944, pages 94, 96

Miki Operation
Troops from Fort Lewis, Washington, landed at Honolulu during First Fleet training in late 1940s, pages 156, 159

Minorities
Rear Admiral Putty Read removed as Chief of Air Technical Training in 1944 after he requested that no more blacks be trained, page 89

Mitscher, Vice Admiral Marc A., USN (USNA, 1910)
Gives Bogan his first plane ride in 1923 at Anacostia, page 29; as Langley (CV-1) air officer in mid-1920s, angered by Commander Aircraft Battle Force, Captain J.M. Reeves, effort to break a carrier landing record under unfavorable conditions, page 35; at Leyte Gulf in October 1944, pages 109-110; assessed by Bogan, pages 118, 141; Bogan offers his staff to Mitscher when he comes to Randolph (CV-15) in 1945, page 140; presents decoration to Bogan in February 1946, page 150

Monaghan, USS (DD-354)
Lost in a typhoon in December 1944, pages 125-127

Morale
   Secretary of the Navy Matthews solicits opinions from flag officers on Navy morale in early 1949, pages 156-162

Morrow Board
   Bogan supports 1925 decision by this air policy board that only naval aviators command carriers, page 57

Naval Academy, U.S.
   Political overtones of Bogan's appointment in 1912, pages 2-3; Bogan's sports while midshipman, pages 3-4; benefits of education for later career, page 5; quality of instruction, page 5; Bogan's recollections of fellow mids, page 7; attrition in 1910s, page 8; Bogan detached after one year as an instructor in the early 1920s because of a personal matter, page 28

Naval Aviation
   Bogan qualifies as an aviator in the mid-1920s when carrier aviation was just getting started, page 31; Bogan's reason for choosing aviation, page 33; Bogan marvels at modern aviation, page 46; naval aviation cadet program at Pensacola in the late 1930s produced excellent naval officers, pages 58-61
   See also Aircraft Carriers

Naval Aviation Cadet Program (NavCad)
   Quality of cadets at Pensacola in the mid-1930s, pages 58-61

Naval Personnel
   Severe shortage of crews after World War I, page 17
   See GI Bill

New Jersey, USS (BB-62)
   Admiral Halsey's flagship attacked in November 1944, page 120; Halsey shows Bogan color movie of attack on Intrepid (CV-11) at Christmas dinner in 1944, pages 121-122, 128-129

News Media
   See Media

Nimitz, Admiral Chester W., USN (USNA, 1905)
   Message to Halsey during Leyte Gulf action in October 1944, page 110

Nurses
   Attended Bogan in the spring of 1943 in the South Pacific, pages 82, 84

O'Callahan, Lieutenant Commander Joseph, CHC, USNR
   Chaplain praised for actions when Franklin (CV-13) was attacked on 19 March 1945, page 133

Odessa, Soviet Union
   U.S. destroyer Broome (DD-210) evacuated refugees from there in 1920, pages 26-27

Okinawa
  USS Franklin (CV-13) prepares for Okinawa campaign in early 1945, page 131; USS Randolph (CV-15) operates in support of troops ashore, pages 139, 145
  See also Task Group 38.3

Pearl Harbor
  Bogan recalls how he heard the news of the December 1941 attack, pages 76-77; Bogan assumes command of Saratoga (CV-3) dry-docked at Pearl Harbor in October 1942, pages 78-79; Bogan takes leave here in early 1945, page 131

Pecos, USS (AO-6)
  Sent to retrieve U.S. personnel from Russian Island after Bolshevik takeover in 1922, page 21

Pensacola Naval Air Station
  See Aviation Training

Philippine Sea, USS (CV-47)
  Takes Bogan to Guantanamo on training cruise in 1947, page 154

Philippines
  Task Force 58 operates in Philippine area in late 1944, page 105; operations in late 1944, pages 114-115; Intrepid planes diverted to Tacloban after ship is attacked in late 1944, pages 117-118; naval support around the Philippines in early 1945, page 129
  See also Leyte Gulf, Battle of

Pirie, Captain Robert E., USN (USNA, 1926)
  Bogan's VF-3 squadron mate assessed, page 43; as superintendent of training at Pensacola in the early 1940s, questions British pilot on his background, page 73; assesses damage to Fanshaw Bay (CVE-70) after Japanese air attack in mid-1944, pages 101-102

Polish-Russian War
  Broome (DD-210) in Riga in 1920 at end of war, pages 25-27

Radford, Admiral Arthur W., USN (USNA, 1916)
  As Commander in Chief Pacific Fleet in 1949, forwards letter from Bogan to Secretary of the Navy Matthews concerning morale along with his personal endorsement of Bogan, page 157

Radio Communications
  Importance of U.S. radio setup at Russian Island in the early 1920s, pages 19-22

Randolph, USS (CV-15)
  Bogan's intended flagship hit by kamikaze on 11 March 1945, page 131; hit by Army P-38 in early 1945, pages 137-138; part of Magic Carpet operation at end of war, pages 138, 147

Read, Rear Admiral Albert C., USN (USNA, 1907)
  Removed as Chief of Air Technical Training in Chicago in 1944 after pressure from Eleanor Roosevelt, page 89

Reeves, Captain Joseph M., USN (USNA, 1894)
  As Commander Aircraft Battle Force in the mid-1920s, credited with making naval aviation a more cohesive force, page 34; unfamiliarity with aviation shown in instances when he made unreasonable demands of Langley (CV-1) pilots, pages 34-38

Rescues
  Bogan is rescued by Aroostook (CM-3) in the mid-1920s after an unsuccessful landing attempt on Langley (CV-1), pages 35-36

Roosevelt, Eleanor
  Precipitates Rear Admiral Putty Read's removal as Chief of Air Technical Training in Chicago in 1944 because of race-related comments he made, page 89

Royal Navy
  High fatality rate for fleet air arm pilots training at Naval Air Station Miami in the early 1940s, pages 72-73

Russia
  Polish-Russian War, page 25
  See Bolsheviks; Russian Island

Russian Island
  Background of U.S. presence here in the early 1920s, pages 18-20; importance to U.S., page 19; U.S. turns station over to Bolsheviks in 1922, pages 20-22

Saipan
  Involvement of escort carriers of Carrier Division 25 providing air support for land operations in 1944, pages 94-104

Sallada, Rear Admiral Harold B., USN (USNA, 1917)
  Carrier division commander in mid-1944 Saipan action, pages 99, 103-104

Santa Fe, USS (CL-60)
  After assisting in fire-fighting effort on Franklin (CV-13) in March 1945, Santa Fe crew member was found to have stolen money, page 135

Saratoga, USS (CV-3)
  Carrier which made successful mock attack on Hawaii in early 1932, pages 44-46; discipline aboard compared to Lexington (CV-2) in the early 1930s, pages 54-55; leaves dry dock at Pearl Harbor and patrols off Guadalcanal in fall of 1942, pages 78-81; Bogan injured by fall from flight deck, pages 81-84

Sherman, Admiral Forrest P., USN (USNA, 1918)
  Chief of Naval Operations Sherman refuses to intercede on Bogan's behalf when he is demoted and nudged into early

retirement in early 1950, page 162; influence with Fleet Admiral Nimitz, page 163

Sherman, Rear Admiral Frederick C., USN (USNA, 1910)
As Commander Task Group 38.3 at October 1944 Leyte Gulf action, pages 108, 114; in action on 25 November 1944, page 120; flies from Task Group 38.3 cruiser to surrender ceremony in September 1945, page 148

Sixth Fleet, U.S.
Created in the late 1940s, pages 151-153; patrols in Mediterranean as deterrent to Russians, page 153

Solace, USS (AH-5)
Bogan treated in Solace after fall from Saratoga (CV-3) flight deck in early 1943, page 82

Soviet Union
U.S. destroyer Broome (DD-210) evacuated refugees from Odessa, Ukraine, in 1920, pages 26-27
See also Russian Island

Spence, USS (DD-512)
Lost in typhoon in December 1944, pages 125-127

Sprague, Rear Admiral Clifton A.F., USN (USNA, 1918)
Bogan split Task Group 38.3 with Sprague right before Japanese surrender in 1945 for more extensive operations, page 147

Sprague, Vice Admiral Thomas L., USN (USNA, 1918)
Relieves Bogan, prematurely and under protest, as Commander First Fleet in early 1950, page 162

Stribling, USS (DD-96)
Eastern Mediterranean cruise in 1919, pages 13-14; officer complement in 1919, page 15

Sturges, Lieutenant Benjamin R., USNR
Quick thinking saves Intrepid (CV-11) planes after kamikaze attack in late 1944, pages 116-117

Submarine Warfare
Evidence of success of submarines off France during World War I, page 10
See Antisubmarine warfare

Task Group 34
Not formed as anticipated at Leyte Gulf in October 1944, pages 109-110, 112-113

Task Group 38.2
At Battle of Leyte Gulf, page 107; in the Philippines in early 1945, page 129; operations around Indochina, page 130

Task Group 38.3
  Bogan commands this task group in Okinawa campaign in mid-1945, page 142; in China Sea in January 1945, page 143; position at time of Japanese surrender, page 147; Bogan decorated for command of Task Group 38.3, pages 149-150

Task Group 58.4
  Provides air support to Guam in 1944, pages 104-105; sweeps around the Philippines, page 105

Tenth Fleet, U.S.
  Explanation of organization in Atlantic in World War II, pages 85-87

Test Pilots
  Bogan tests fighters and bombers at Anacostia in the early 1930s, pages 50-53

Training - Aviation
  See Aviation Training

Turner, Vice Admiral Richmond Kelly, USN (USNA, 1908)
  As Commander Task Force 51 congratulates Bogan on his victory at Saipan in 1944, page 97

Typhoon
  Halsey sends ships through typhoon near the Philippines on 18 December 1944 despite warning from Bogan, pages 125-128

Ulithi
  Houston (CL-81) towed in after October 1944 torpedo attack, page 106; used for refueling and reprovisioning, page 107; site of training for elements of Task Force 38 in March 1945, pages 138-139

Van Deurs, Ensign George, USN (USNA, 1921A)
  Gives Bogan one of his first plane rides in the early 1920s, pages 29-30; as commanding officer of Philippine Sea (CV-47) in 1947, takes Bogan on training cruise to Guantanamo, pages 154-155

War Games
  VF-1 takes part in mock attack on Oahu in February 1932, pages 44-45

Wasp, USS (CV-18)
  Takes on survivors from Franklin (CV-13) in March 1945, page 133

Weather
  See Typhoon; Cold Weather Training

White Plains, USS (CVE-66)
  Bogan's flagship as a carrier division commander in 1944 considered a dud, pages 94, 96, 150

Wilbur, Curtis D.
  Riding in California (BB-44) as Secretary of the Navy in mid-1920s, entertained with air demonstration ordered by Commander Aircraft Battle Force, Captain J.M. Reeves, at peril to VF-1 pilots flying in bad weather, pages 37-38

Windsor, Duke of
  Had little power while serving as Governor of the Bahamas in World War II, page 75

Winston, Lieutenant Commander Francis L, USN
  Bogan praises his fighter director officer, killed when the Franklin (CV-13) was attacked on 19 March 1945, page 132

World War I
  Submarine warfare, page 10; convoys, pages 10-11; severe personnel shortage after armistice signed, page 17

Yarnell, Rear Admiral Harry E., USN (USNA, 1897)
  Assessed as Commander Aircraft Battle Force in the early 1930s, pages 44-45

Yorktown, USS (CV-5)
  Participates in Caribbean fleet exercise in the late 1930s, pages 64, 66; sent to the Pacific coast in preparation for war, pages 64, 70; Rear Admiral W.F. Halsey angered in the late 1930s by indecisiveness on the part of Yorktown's skipper, Captain Ernest McWhorter, pages 65-68; fleet exercise in Honolulu and dry-docking at Bremerton in 1939, page 71

COMMANDER FIRST TASK FLEET
UNITED STATES PACIFIC FLEET
FLAGSHIP OF THE COMMANDER

A7-1/00-wgt

Serial:

C-O-N-F-I-D-E-N-T-I-A-L

From: Vice Admiral Gerald F. BOGAN, U.S. Navy, 9628.
To: The Secretary of the Navy.
Via: (1) Commander in Chief, U.S. Pacific Fleet.
(2) The Chief of Naval Operations.

Subject: Comment on statement of Captain John G. CROMMELIN, U.S. Navy, 57979.

Reference: (a) SecNav conf. dispatch 142122.
(b) Article 1245, U.S. Navy Regulations.

My dear Mr. Secretary:

At the beginning it is proper for me to state that in no manner have I, to date, endorsed or condemned Captain Crommelin's statement because no one has asked me to do so. Had such been the case honest necessity and conscience would have required hearty and complete agreement with the affirmations made in his release to or interview with the press.

Your dispatch, which prompts this letter, is surprising in its interpretation of the motive in the basic statement. It avers that the Crommelin statement and subsequent public utterances have embarrassed the progress of unification and harmony and the Navy Department. It further states that these remarks have been inspired by apprehensions concerning the future of Naval Aviation. Mr. Secretary, while realizing that this is your honest belief, that interpretation of the genesis of Crommelin's release is the most superficial gloss and does not remotely touch the heart of the question. The basic reason behind all of it is a genuine fear in the Navy for the security of our country if the policies followed in the Department of Defense since the National Security Act became law are not drastically changed, and soon.

It is necessary for me to assert now to you that I opposed the act as written and passed and so testified before the committee. My reasons for opposition and suggestions for other methods of achieving ultimate unity in the Military Establishment were given at that time, 1 July 1947. I forecast much of what subsequently occurred. Records of that testimony are available. The creation of three Departments or sub Departments where formerly there were but two is not unification. Under the present law it can be made to and does operate effectively in the field. But it would be sheer balderdash to assume that there has been anything approaching it among the Secretariat, the Joint Staff, or

- 1 -

COMMANDER FIRST TASK FLEET
UNITED STATES PACIFIC FLEET
FLAGSHIP OF THE COMMANDER

A7-1/00-wgt

Serial:

C-O-N-F-I-D-E-N-T-I-A-L

Subject: Comment on statement of Captain John G. CROMMELIN, U.S. Navy, 57979.

----

the high command of all three services. Knowing that honest differences of opinion must constantly be present, bickering is still the rule; unanimity is non-existent.

The morale of the Navy is lower today than at any time since I entered the commissioned ranks in 1916. Lowered morale, to some degree, may be expected to follow any war during the readjustment to the organization for peace. In my opinion this descent, almost to despondency, stems from complete confusion as to the future role of the Navy and its advantages or disadvantages as a permanent career. Optimistic letters and plans issue from Washington. And concurrently the situation deteriorates with each press release. The younger men are necessarily concerned with their future security. We of greater age, and, we hope, more mature judgment are fearful that the country is being, if it has not already been, sold a false bill of goods. Junior officers in large numbers, whose confidence I enjoy, have come to me asking advice on their future course of action. I have invariably encouraged them to enhance their professional ability against the day when the troublesome questions now paramount would be equably resolved. It is becoming increasingly difficult for me to do this honestly.

If the adequate Military or Defense Establishment could be achieved without a Navy and Naval Aviation, I would gladly advocate using funds now expended to maintain that service, on the procurement of the best other necessary weapons and equipment. Not even the United States can support indefinitely, during peace, the tragically large military budgets we are now devouring.

There is no cheap quick victory possible between any two nations or groups of nations each having strong even if relatively unequal power. Yet at a time as potentially critical as ever existed during our history, the public has been lured into complacency by irresponsible speeches by advocates of this theory. The result could be a great national and worldwide catastrophe.

COMMANDER FIRST TASK FLEET
UNITED STATES PACIFIC FLEET
FLAGSHIP OF THE COMMANDER

A7-1/00-wgt

Serial:

C-O-N-F-I-D-E-N-T-I-A-L

Subject: Comment on statement of Captain John G. CROMMELIN, U.S. Navy, 57979.

     I have been informed that when the committee hearings resume in October the Navy will be afforded the opportunity to state its case completely on the items comprising the agenda. Since Captain Crommelin's press statement, I am more optimistic than before that such will be the case. But the agenda does not cover the fundamentals of our National Security. It embraces a total of eight items, all pertinent but by no means the complete whole. It is my earnest hope that at some time in the near future this vital subject may be thoroughly explored with no consideration being given to the reputations nor politics of the witnesses who appear. It is bigger than personalities, broader and deeper than politics. It is our country.

                                                    Respectfully,

                                                   G. F. BOGAN.

First Endorsement
on Vice Admiral G.F. Bogan's
Conf. ltr ser 0183 of 20 Sept 1949

From: Commander in Chief Pacific Fleet
To: Secretary of the Navy

Subj: Comment on statement of Captain John G. Crommelin
U.S. Navy, 57979

1. Forwarded

2. Vice Admiral Bogan is an officer of great ability and wide experience in Naval Aviation and Naval Warfare. There is no question of his sincereity and high principles. I know that the writing of his letter was motivated by sincere patriotism.

3. Right or wrong, the majority of officers in the Pacific Fleet concur with Capt Crommelin and with the ideas of Vice Admiral Bogan above. Most will avoid any statements to that effect and they would probably question the propriety of and timing of such public statements. Nevertheless it would be a grave mistake to underestimate the depth and sincerity of their feelings.

4. Because of my conviction that this letter is representative of the general feeling, I commend it to your attention.

A.W. Radford

C-O-P-Y

A7-1
Ser 03P00
Op-00/mm

C-O-N-F-I-D-E-N-T-I-A-L   28 September 1949

SECOND ENDORSEMENT on
Vice Admiral G. F. Bogan's
Conf. ltr ser 0183 of 20
September 1949

From: Chief of Naval Operations
To :   Secretary of the Navy

Subject: Comment on statement of Captain John G. CROMMELIN,
          U. S. Navy, 57979.

    1.   Forwarded.

    2.   I concur in the endorsement of Commander in Chief, Pacific Fleet. Naval officers have faith in the Navy and a knowledge of the aggressive role it plays in the defense of the country. They are convinced that a Navy stripped of its offensive power means a nation stripped of its offensive power.

    3.   I believe that Fleet Admiral King in October 1945 summed up the present Navy-wide concern when in a report he stated, ". . . . . . seapower will not be accorded adequate recognition, because the organization contemplated would permit reduction of that seapower by individuals who are not thoroughly familiar with its potentialities, as has happened in several other countries. France never used her navy to good advantage. The German General Staff failed, in two wars, to appreciate the potency of seapower. The absorption of Britain's crack Royal Naval Air Service into an independent Royal Air Force and the consequent withering of her naval aviation left her in 1941 a second rate navy. Another significant fact is that Japan's collapse was coincident with the reduction of her seapower -- at the end of the war she was stronger on the ground and in the air than at the start, but her navy was practically eliminated. It follows that if the navy's welfare is one of the prerequisites to the nation's welfare - and I sincerely believe that to be the case - any step that is not good for the navy is not good for the nation."

                                                  LOUIS DENFELD

cc: CinCpac
    Com1st Task Flt.   C-O-N-F-I-D-E-N-T-I-A-L

www.ingramcontent.com/pod-product-compliance
Lightning Source LLC
Chambersburg PA
CBHW082208070526
44585CB00020B/2328